Discrimination & Prejudice

Understanding Obesity

Big Portions, Big Problems

Discrimination & Prejudice

Emotions & Eating

Exercise for Fitness & Weight Loss

Fast Food & the Obesity Epidemic

Health Issues Caused by Obesity

Looking & Feeling Good in Your Body

Nature & Nurture: The Causes of Obesity

No Quick Fix: Fad Diets & Weight-Loss Miracles

Surgery & Medicine for Weight Loss

Discrimination & Prejudice

Autumn Libal

Mason Crest

Mason Crest
450 Parkway Drive, Suite D
Broomall, PA 19008
www.masoncrest.com

Copyright © 2015 by Mason Crest, an imprint of National Highlights, Inc. All rights reserved. No part of this publication may be reproduced or transmitted in any form or by any means, electronic or mechanical, including photocopying, recording, taping, or any information storage and retrieval system, without permission from the publisher.

Printed in the United States of America.

Series ISBN: 978-1-4222-3056-5
ISBN: 978-1-4222-3058-9
ebook ISBN: 978-1-4222-8841-2

Cataloging-in-Publication Data on file with the Library of Congress.

Contents

Introduction / 7

1. Two Epidemics / 9

2. Not All Bodies Are the Same / 23

3. The Poor Get Fat, the Rich Get Thin? / 41

4. Big Targets: Advertising and America's Obesity Epidemic / 57

5. Life Is Different if You're "Fat" / 71

6. No Easy Answers / 85

Series Glossary of Key Terms / 98

Further Reading / 100

For More Information / 101

Index / 102

Picture Credits / 103

About the Author and the Consultant / 104

KEY ICONS TO LOOK FOR:

Text-Dependent Questions: These questions send the reader back to the text for more careful attention to the evidence presented there.

Words to Understand: These words with their easy-to-understand definitions will increase the reader's understanding of the text, while building vocabulary skills.

Series Glossary of Key Terms: This back-of-the book glossary contains terminology used throughout this series. Words found here increase the reader's ability to read and comprehend higher-level books and articles in this field.

Research Projects: Readers are pointed toward areas of further inquiry connected to each chapter. Suggestions are provided for projects that encourage deeper research and analysis.

Sidebars: This boxed material within the main text allows readers to build knowledge, gain insights, explore possibilities, and broaden their perspectives by weaving together additional information to provide realistic and holistic perspectives.

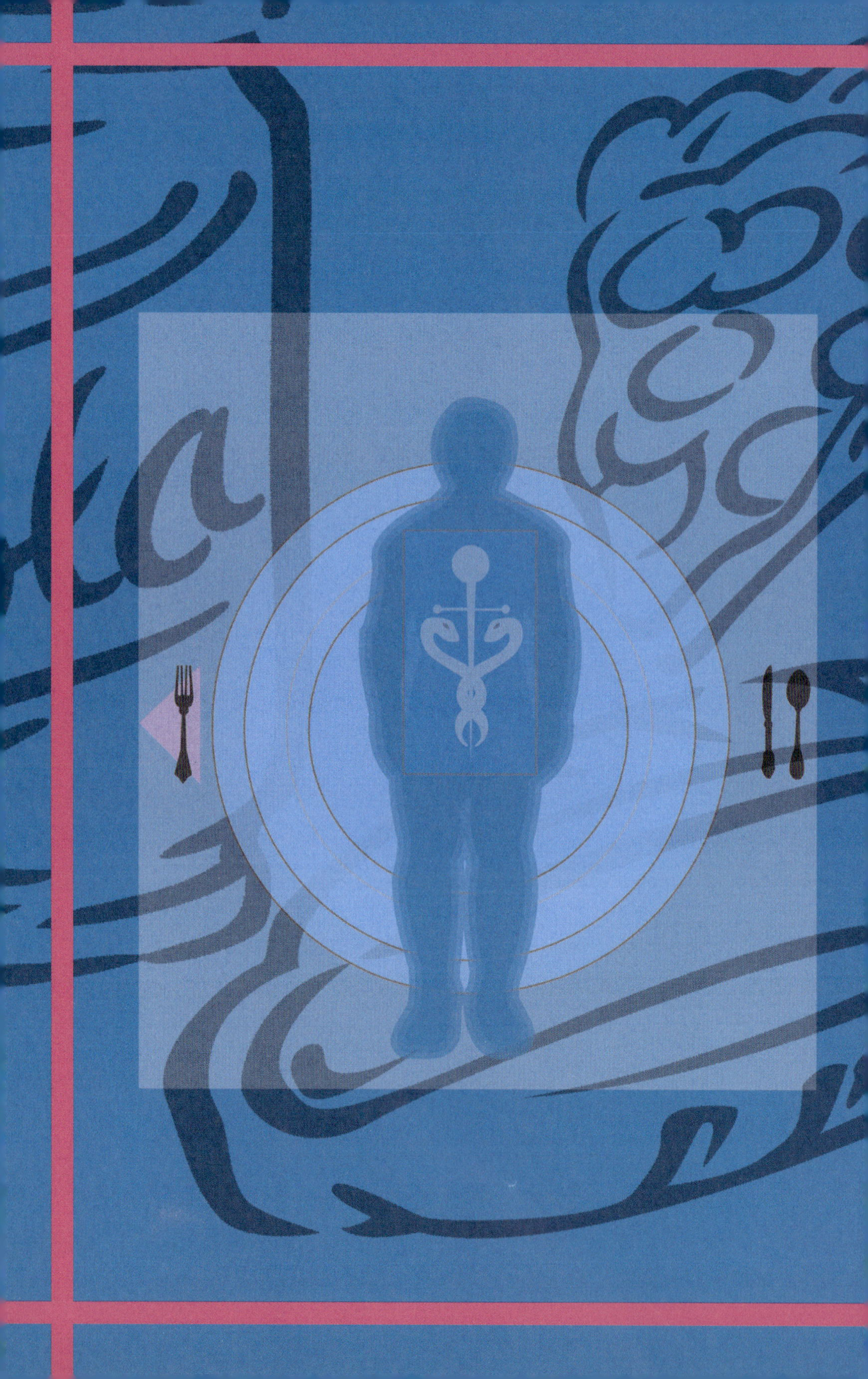

Introduction

We as a society often reserve our harshest criticism for those conditions we understand the least. Such is the case with obesity. Obesity is a chronic and often-fatal disease that accounts for 300,000 deaths each year. It is second only to smoking as a cause of premature death in the United States. People suffering from obesity need understanding, support, and medical assistance. Yet what they often receive is scorn.

Today, children are the fastest growing segment of the obese population in the United States. This constitutes a public health crisis of enormous proportions. Living with childhood obesity affects self-esteem, employment, and attainment of higher education. But childhood obesity is much more than a social stigma. It has serious health consequences.

Childhood obesity increases the risk for poor health in adulthood and premature death. Depression, diabetes, asthma, gallstones, orthopedic diseases, and other obesity-related conditions are all on the rise in children. Over the last 20 years, more children are being diagnosed with type 2 diabetes—a leading cause of preventable blindness, kidney failure, heart disease, stroke, and amputations. Obesity is undoubtedly the most pressing nutritional disorder among young people today.

This series is an excellent first step toward understanding the obesity crisis and profiling approaches for remedying it. If we are to reverse obesity's current trend, there must be family, community, and national objectives promoting healthy eating and exercise. As a nation, we must demand broad-based public-health initiatives to limit TV watching, curtail junk food advertising toward children, and promote physical activity. More than rhetoric, these need to be our rallying cry. Anything short of this will eventually fail, and within our lifetime obesity will become the leading cause of death in the United States if not in the world.

Victor F. Garcia, M.D.
Founder, Bariatric Surgery Center
Cincinnati Children's Hospital Medical Center
Professor of Pediatrics and Surgery
School of Medicine
University of Cincinnati

Words to Understand

cultural: Relating to the characteristics (like practices, belief systems, types of food, art, etc.) that define or are particular to a group of people.
paradox: Something that seems to be contradictory but is or may be true.
affluent: Having a lot of money or possessions.
Calories: The amount of energy needed to raise the temperature of 1 kilogram of pure water by one degree Celsius; calorie with a lowercase "c" is the amount of energy needed to raise the temperature of 1 gram of pure water by one degree Celsius.
sedentary: Not requiring much motion.
type 2 diabetes: A common form of diabetes characterized by an inefficient production of or use of insulin.
osteoarthritis: A form of arthritis characterized by a gradual loss of cartilage between the joints.
detrimental: Causing harm or damage.
social: Relating to society.
stigmatization: The process of labeling someone or something as socially undesirable.
anecdotal: Based on secondhand, nonscientific information.
stereotyped: Judged based on generalizations.
ignorance: Lack of knowledge.

Chapter 1

Two Epidemics

- An Epidemic of Body-Hate
- An Epidemic of Obesity
- The Acceptable Prejudice

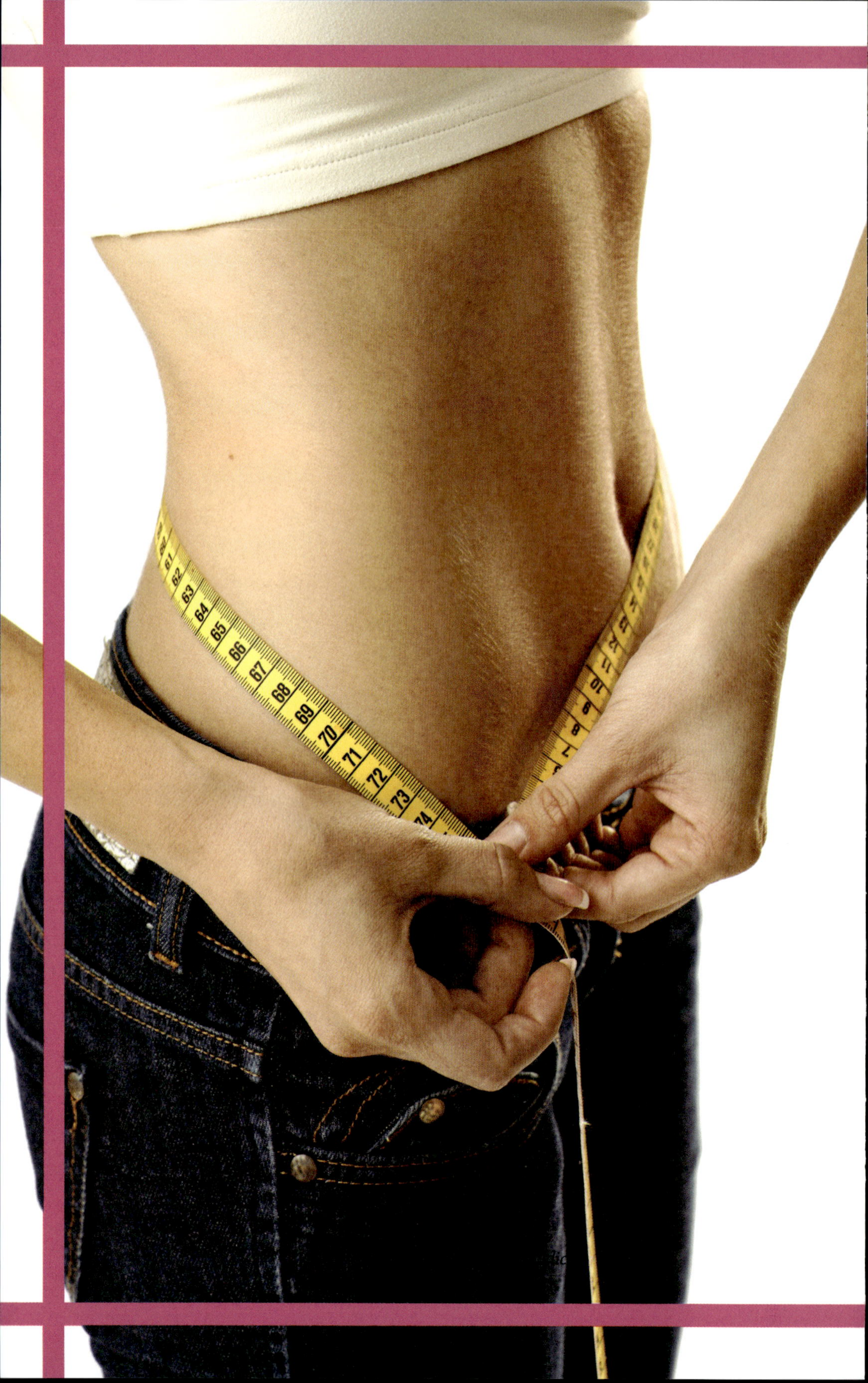

The human body is a beautiful, amazing thing. More complex than any computer, better built than any machine, the human body is a marvel of abilities and mystery. It is your fundamental vehicle for life. Every moment of your existence, your body performs complicated tasks that not only keep you alive but also allow you to think, feel, communicate, work, play, and more. With proper maintenance (and a bit of luck) the human body can continue performing these tasks for fifty, seventy, one hundred, or even more years. With people living longer than ever before, and with athletes continuing to set world records, we see that the human body's true limits have yet to be discovered.

Unfortunately, many people don't realize how wonderful their own and other people's bodies are. In our society, disrespect for people's bodies, even body-hate, is far too common. Many people find it difficult, even impossible, to give their own bodies the love and respect they deserve, and some people think it is perfectly acceptable to make judgments about, even discriminate against, others based on the way their bodies look.

An Epidemic of Body-Hate

Think for a moment about the following statistics. According to a study done by *SHAPE Magazine*, more than 80 percent of women between the ages of 25 and 54 are dissatisfied with their bodies. Similarly, 81 percent of ten-year-old children are afraid of being fat. Unhappiness with one's body appears to affect younger children as well. A shocking 42 percent of first- through third-grade girls want to be thinner. Statistics like these make a striking statement. They say that an awful lot of people in America dislike their bodies and wish they could change the way they look.

Our feelings toward our bodies are influenced by many sources. In fact, every day you are bombarded by messages telling you that your body should

Two Epidemics / 11

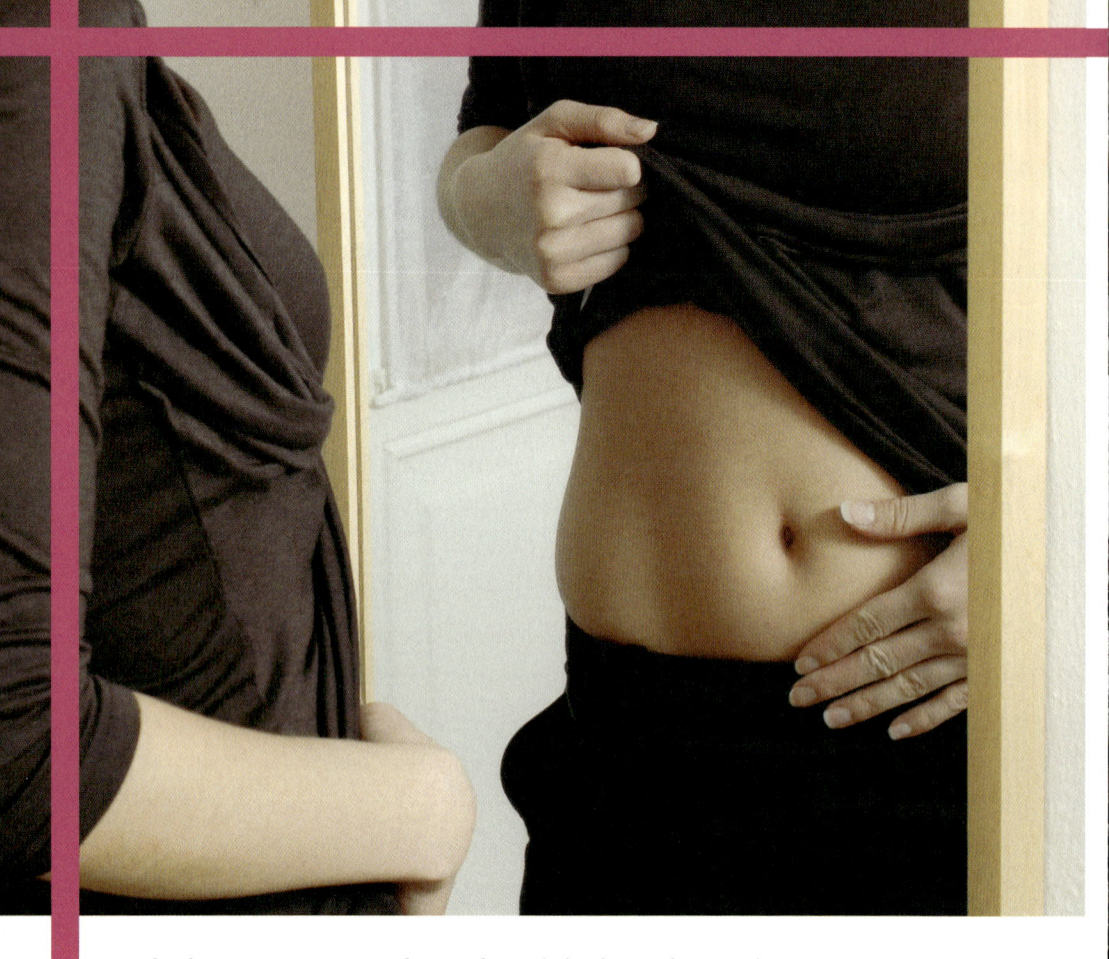

look a certain way or that it doesn't look good enough. Walk down the checkout aisle at the grocery story. Turn on the television for ten minutes. Flip through a fashion magazine, or look at the advertisements hanging in storefronts. It's pretty clear what a beautiful body is supposed to look like. Women are supposed to be tall and thin with perfect skin, voluptuous breasts, and long, flowing hair. Men are also supposed to be tall with perfect skin and hair, and every muscle in their bodies should appear as though chiseled out of stone. And one thing is very clear: A "beautiful" body should not have an ounce of visible fat!

It is a sad reality, but the look so many Americans value, desire, and strive for is completely unrealistic. All over America, men and women are starving themselves, exercising religiously, spending huge amounts of money, and hating their bodies for something that only exists in pictures. Today, even stars can't obtain our culture's ideals of beauty. Models and actors suffer from eating disorders; athletes take steroids or other muscle-building substances; famous and wealthy people have access to dieticians, personal trainers, professional makeup artists, and plastic surgeons; and still their photographs are airbrushed and digitally enhanced to create the picture of beauty envied by so many. Despite these facts, most people still feel a great deal of dissatisfaction with themselves for not living up to these **cultural** ideals and wish they could change their bodies. Many Americans are suffering from body-hate. They find the slightest physical "flaw" or ounce of fat abhorrent in themselves and equally unacceptable in others.

An Epidemic of Obesity

Americans may be striving for the slender, "perfect" body, but there is little evidence to suggest they are succeeding in this quest. In fact, the opposite seems to be happening: Americans are getting larger all the time. Consider these statistics. According to the Centers for Disease Control and Prevention (CDC), childhood obesity has tripled in adolescents over the last 30 years and more than one in three children are overweight or obese. The numbers (along with our waistlines) just keep growing. In America today, obesity, the state of being very overweight, is a crisis that is quickly becoming an American way of life.

America's obesity epidemic is difficult for many people to understand. It seems like a **paradox**. How can Americans be so obsessed with thinness and beauty on the one hand and as a population fail so miserably to control their weight on the other? Certainly many things are contributing to the obesity epidemic. Some of these things are within and others are outside of the average individual's control.

Two Epidemics / 13

14 / Discrimination & Prejudice

> *Whether it is as a driver or a passenger, Americans, on average, spend more than 18 hours in their cars per week.*

Americans live in an **affluent**, technologically advanced society. This gives Americans greater access than ever before to food, products, conveniences, and services—all things that have the potential to make the population healthier. Great health strides have been made. Some diseases like smallpox and polio have been almost completely eliminated from the country, and treatments for many potentially fatal conditions have extended life like never before. However, America's comfortable lifestyle has health trappings as well. Today, Americans rely heavily on prepared, prepackaged, fast foods for many of their meals—foods that are high in **Calories**, fat, salt, and sugar. Americans spend hours every week traveling in cars instead of walking or riding a bicycle. A huge portion of the population works at desks or in **sedentary** environments instead of at physical labor. The majority of people rely on entertainment from televisions and computers to fill much of their leisure time instead of engaging in sports, outdoor recreation, or other energy-burning activities. While all these things have their positive and convenient sides, they also contribute to increasing weight and decreasing health.

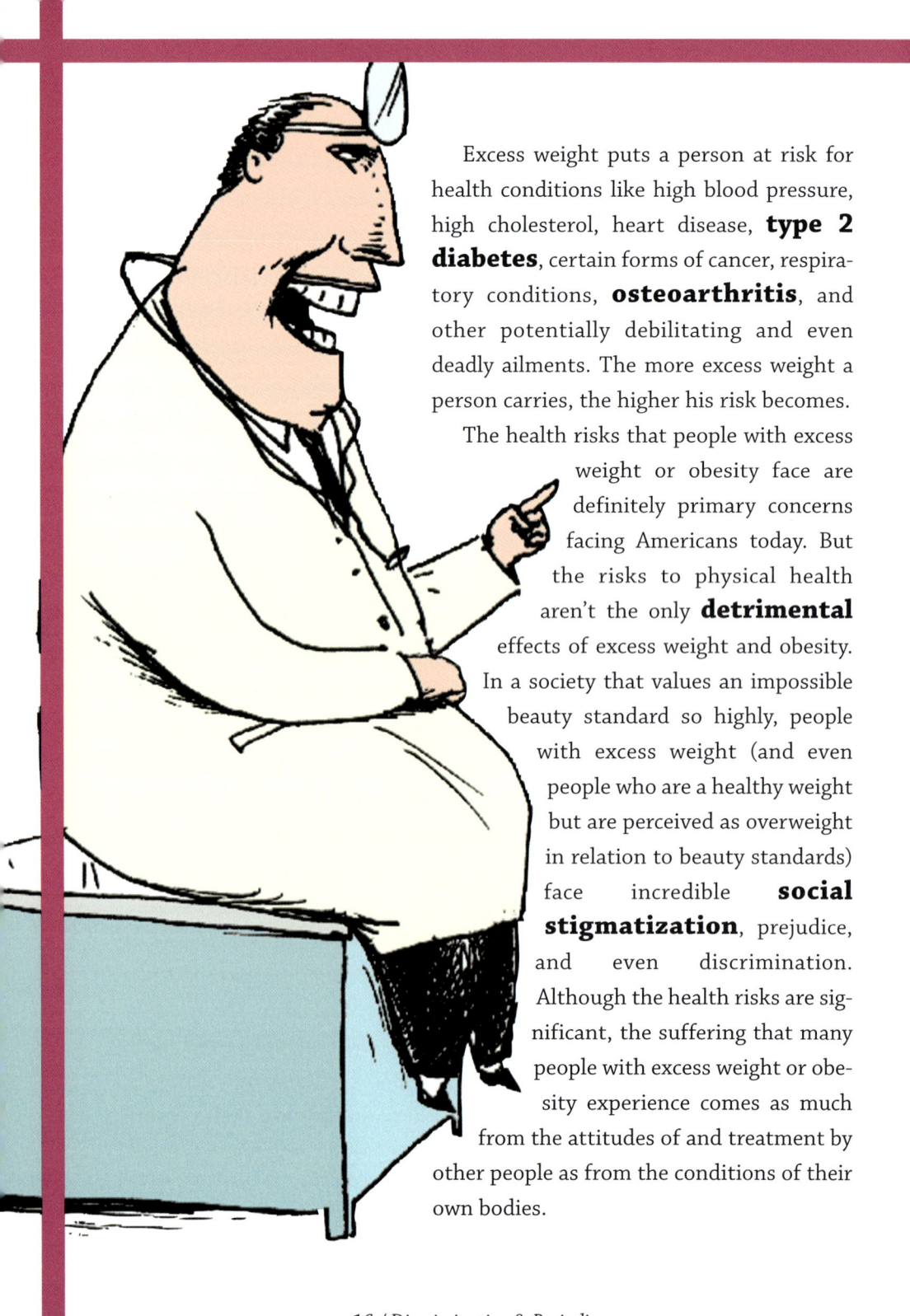

Excess weight puts a person at risk for health conditions like high blood pressure, high cholesterol, heart disease, **type 2 diabetes**, certain forms of cancer, respiratory conditions, **osteoarthritis**, and other potentially debilitating and even deadly ailments. The more excess weight a person carries, the higher his risk becomes. The health risks that people with excess weight or obesity face are definitely primary concerns facing Americans today. But the risks to physical health aren't the only **detrimental** effects of excess weight and obesity. In a society that values an impossible beauty standard so highly, people with excess weight (and even people who are a healthy weight but are perceived as overweight in relation to beauty standards) face incredible **social stigmatization**, prejudice, and even discrimination. Although the health risks are significant, the suffering that many people with excess weight or obesity experience comes as much from the attitudes of and treatment by other people as from the conditions of their own bodies.

The Acceptable Prejudice

Discrimination is the act of treating some people differently than other people because of factors or characteristics (such as appearance) that have nothing to do with their abilities and potentials. People with excess weight are often treated differently, and numerous **anecdotal** accounts and an ever-growing number of scientific studies suggest that weight discrimination is real and prevalent in American

Two Epidemics / 17

society. Young children are discriminated against when they are denied friendship or made fun of simply because they are large. Students with excess weight or obesity are being discriminated against when there are no desks in their classroom that are comfortable. People are discriminated against when they are denied health insurance coverage for weight-related medical treatments or when they are passed over for promotion because their supervisors disapprove of their size.

Discrimination based on body size is often called the last acceptable prejudice. Americans as a whole have rejected many other forms of prejudice as unacceptable in a tolerant, democratic society. The U.S. Congress passed the Civil Rights Act of 1964 to ensure people have equal access to voting rights, public spaces, public education, federally funded programs, employment, and other resources regardless of their race, color, religion, sex, or national origin. Over the years, our ideas of rights, justice, and equal opportunities have expanded even more. Many private company policies as well as local, state, and federal laws now also reject discrimination on additional grounds such as physical disabilities, beliefs, or sexual orientation.

Despite this progress, people with excess weight or obesity will still find little protection from discrimination either under the law or from society as a whole. While American society has made many advances in recognizing people's inherent rights and value, cruel treatment and discrimination toward individuals for their body size is still common and largely accepted. Fat jokes can be heard from the school ground to network television. Weight-based insults abound. Many doctors continue to resist providing adequate medical counseling and care for overweight and obese patients, and obese persons continue to be **stereotyped** as lazy, indulgent, weak-willed, sad, unclean, and unlovable.

American society's overwhelming emphasis on a particularly narrow (and unachievable) beauty standard is partly to blame for creating a hostile living environment for people who are overweight or obese. A popular media filled with the thin and apparently flawless leaves the average American with few, if any, realistic role models and reinforces the notion that to be anything other than "perfect" is unacceptable. But **ignorance** may be as much to blame for judgmental and discriminatory notions about people with excess weight as any other factor. Despite the fact that the majority of American adults are now overweight and obesity rates are growing all the time, most Americans still don't understand the true causes of severe weight gain. People continue to believe that individuals who are overweight or obese have brought their conditions on themselves and are therefore completely to blame. These attitudes bring suffering to people struggling with excess weight and do nothing to improve health or well-being.

Prejudice is based on ignorance, and plenty of people are ignorant about what obesity is and what causes it. Many people assume that if

Research Project

Choose two of the conditions that people with overweight or obesity are at greater risk of developing. Use the CDC website (www.cdc.gov) or other online resources to see what this increased risk is. How much more likely is the condition for someone who is obese than someone who is not? How might the two connections be connected?

someone appears to be carrying extra pounds, he is an overeating couch potato. This is simply not true. Bodies are much more complicated than that, and different bodies work in different ways. Before addressing the

Make Connections: Overweight

You are probably used to the word "overweight" being used as an adjective to describe someone, as in the sentence, "He is overweight." In medical use, however, overweight is also used as a noun; it is a medical condition. In this usage, it would be perfectly appropriate to say, "He has overweight," or, "A person with overweight," the same way one might say, "He has asthma," or, "A person with arthritis."

> **Text-Dependent Questions:**
>
> 1. What percentage of women says that they are dissatisfied with their bodies?
> 2. According to the CDC, how many children are overweight or obese?
> 3. Name three factors that have contributed to the rise of overweight and obesity in America.
> 4. Name two conditions that someone who is obese is at a higher risk of developing.
> 5. What is "the last acceptable prejudice"?

types of discrimination people who are overweight or obese face, we need to understand what "overweight" and "obesity" are. Many people just look at another person's body and make a judgment about whether that person is "acceptable," overweight, obese, or some other body-size category. These judgments, however, are based entirely on appearance, and excess weight and obesity can actually have little to do with appearance. "Overweight" and "obese" are actually medical terms, and they have medical criteria for their use.

Two Epidemics / 21

Words to Understand

objective: Free of bias, based on facts.
genetics: A branch of biology dealing with heredity and the mechanisms by which characteristics are transferred from one generation to the next.
admonished: Criticized for doing or not doing something.
fiber: The coarse material found in grains, fruits, and vegetables that aids digestion.
metabolism: Chemical interactions taking place in living organisms to provide the energy and nutrients needed to sustain life.

chapter 2

Not All Bodies Are the Same

- Understanding Overweight and Obesity

- Weight Gain: A Simple Formula, a Complicated Issue

- A World of Difference

Understanding Overweight and Obesity

So what determines whether a person is overweight or obese? On the one hand, magazines, movies, television shows, and other media sources show us images of ridiculously thin people. These images are neither realistic nor healthy, and those who wish to obtain these stick-thin bodies often have a skewed understanding of what a healthy body should look like. On the other hand, millions of Americans are overweight, and when seeing overweight bodies every day, we may begin to see these bodies as the norm. But being overweight is not healthy either, and when constantly faced with these two extremes—too thin and too heavy—a person can quickly lose sight of what a healthy body should look like. When discussing overweight and obesity, we must remember that the most important thing is not to achieve a specific look. The most important thing is to achieve good health.

Many people think weight is an **objective** standard of whether or not a person is healthy, but this is a myth. Since bodies come in all different shapes and sizes, it's impossible to pick a weight that is healthy for everyone. No one can say, "One hundred thirty pounds is the optimal weight," or, "One hundred fifty pounds is an unhealthy weight." Except in very extreme cases, it is also impossible to judge whether or not a person is healthy just by looking at her. You can't see things like a person's fitness level or heart health. A very thin person could have a much lower fitness level and unhealthier heart than a much heavier person.

The body size that is healthy for an individual depends on many factors, like the person's height, age, sex, fitness level, and **genetics**. In fact, weight alone isn't a very good measurement of whether a person is a healthy body size or not at all. For example, if you were told that a person weighed 230 pounds, you might immediately assume the person was overweight. But perhaps the person was a six-foot, five-inch-tall male wrestler. In this case, 230 pounds might not be overweight for that person at all. In fact, he might be very athletic and healthy.

Weight alone can't tell us very much about a person's body composition, so doctors rely on other tools when assessing a person's body size and health. Usually these tools try to determine approximately how much of the person's body is made up of fat compared to how much of his body is made up of lean tissue (muscle, bone, organs, and other body tissues).

Not All Bodies Are the Same / 25

The most common tool doctors use to evaluate body size is something called body mass index (BMI). BMI is a mathematical formula that uses weight and height to estimate how much of the person's body is made up of fat and whether the person is a healthy size. If you are under twenty, you will need to go to this website to use one of the charts to determine your BMI: www.cdc.gov/healthyweight/assessing/bmi/childrens_bmi/about_childrens_bmi.html. The formula for people over twenty is as follows:

[Weight in pounds ÷ (Height in inches x Height in inches)] x 703 = BMI

or

[Weight in kilograms ÷ (Height in centimeters x Height in centimeters)] x 10,000 = BMI

BMI does not have one number that is considered healthy and another that is considered unhealthy. Instead, one's BMI is compared to a range of numbers. If a person's BMI formula yields a number below 18.5, a doctor would classify that person as being "underweight" (which can be a serious health threat of its own). A BMI that falls anywhere between 18.5 and 24.9 is considered a "normal" weight. If a person's BMI falls between 25.0 and 29.9, he would be considered "overweight," and a person who has a BMI of 30.0 or above would be classified as "obese." Here is an example for a person who weighs 135 pounds and is five feet four inches (64 inches) tall:

[135 pounds ÷ (64 inches x 64 inches)] x 703 =
23.17 (a "normal" weight)

In American society, many people who are five feet four inches tall and weigh 135 pounds consider themselves overweight because they don't look like the ultra-thin people pictured in the media.

Not All Bodies Are the Same / 27

28 / *Discrimination & Prejudice*

Make Connections: BMI and Muscle

If a person had a high BMI, but his extra body mass came from muscle, we might immediately assume that the person is healthy regardless of his extra size. This could, however, be an erroneous assumption. Muscle tissue may not cause some of the negative health effects that fat tissue causes (like an increase in cholesterol levels and reduction in the effectiveness of insulin, the hormone that regulates blood sugar), but too much of any body tissue can have negative health consequences. This is because the more body mass you have, the harder your heart must work to pump blood through your body. Excess body mass—even if caused by muscle instead of fat—can increase a person's risk of developing left ventricular hypertrophy, a dangerous and potentially deadly condition in which the left ventricle of the heart enlarges from overuse. A very high BMI, therefore, can still indicate that a person is at risk for certain health conditions even if he has little fat tissue.

As you can see, however, their BMI falls well within the range considered normal and healthy for the human body.

Since BMI takes a person's height into account, it is a better measure of a person's body composition than weight alone, but it can still be quite inaccurate for some people. This is because muscle, an extremely dense body tissue, weighs eight to nine times as much as an equal amount of fat, a body tissue that is quite light. In other words, you could have two people of equal height, one with a large amount of muscle and one with a large amount of fat, and the muscular person could actually have a higher BMI than the person with the large amount of fat. In fact, according to the BMI formula, the 230-pound wrestler we discussed earlier would have a BMI of 27.3 and would be considered overweight. His additional poundage, however, could be pure muscle.

Because BMI can overestimate the amount of fat in very muscular people and underestimate the amount of fat in people with very little muscle mass, the National Institutes of Health (NIH) suggests that it should be combined with additional information, like waist circumference and other risk factors, for a more accurate evaluation of a person's overall health. According to the NIH, men whose waists measure over forty inches and women whose waists measure over thirty-five inches are at a greater risk for developing weight-related health problems. Additional risk factors include high blood pressure, cholesterol, triglyceride, or blood-sugar levels; a family

> "Individuals who are obese . . . have a 50 to 100% increased risk of premature death from all causes, compared to individuals with a healthy weight."
> —The U.S. Surgeon General

history of heart disease; physical inactivity; and smoking. A person who has a high BMI, a high waist circumference, and two or more risk factors is at high risk of developing weight-related health problems. A doctor would typically recommend that such a person lose weight and take steps to address other risk factors (by, for example, beginning an exercise program and giving up smoking).

A person who by medical standards is overweight or obese is at a significantly increased risk of all kinds of physical ailments. However, people who are medically overweight or obese as well as people who are judged to be so because their bodies don't conform to beauty standards, are also at an increased risk for depression. Overweight- and obesity-related depression could be due to chemical imbalances within the body, but it could also be linked to the discrimination and low self-esteem that many people suffering from overweight and obesity experience.

So why are our attitudes, not simply toward overweight and obesity as conditions, but to the actual people struggling with these conditions, so negative? One of the major reasons overweight and obese people are discriminated against is because their conditions are seen as their fault. Overweight people, common belief goes, make themselves overweight and should therefore receive no sympathy and should even be **admonished** for their condition. But are such attitudes fair? Should people with excess weight be blamed for their conditions? What causes overweight and obesity?

Weight Gain: A Simple Formula, a Complicated Issue

Weight gain and loss rely on relatively simple formulas related to the amount of energy we take in and use each day. We take in energy by eating. We use a great deal of energy just running our bodies (keeping our

Not All Bodies Are the Same / 31

ChooseMyPlate.gov

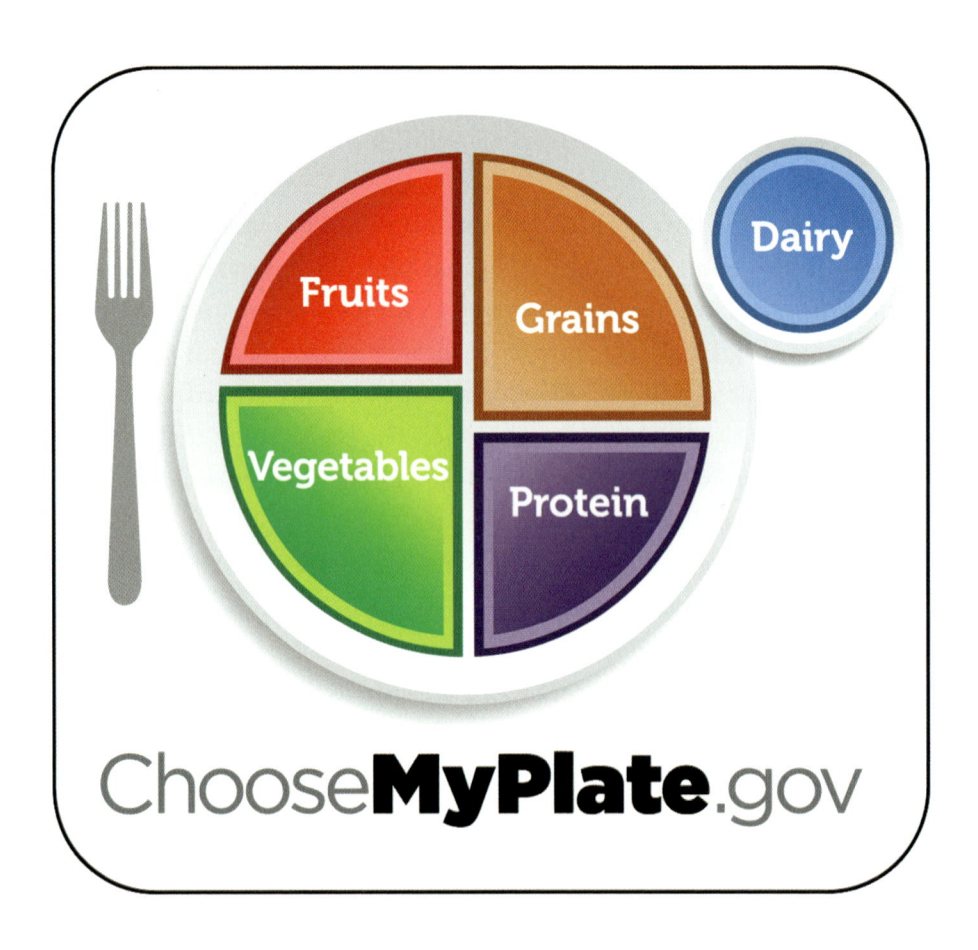

hearts pumping, lungs breathing, brains thinking, body temperature stable, etc.), and we burn even more by performing physical activities. To gain weight, a person must consistently take in more energy each day than she uses. To lose weight, a person must consistently burn more energy each day than she takes in. This would make it seem like people are indeed personally responsible if they gain weight. While a certain amount of personal responsibility is involved in eating and exercising, the issue is really much more complicated than that.

How much energy a person needs each day and where that energy should come from are complicated issues that cause great debate even among health professionals. It's not surprising then that many people have difficulty understanding exactly what and how much they should be eating. For years, Americans relied on something called the Food Guide Pyramid for their nutrition advice. In 2011, the United States Department of Agriculture (USDA) created the MyPlate as an easy-to-understand reference tool, and since then it has been promoted as the ultimate model for healthy eating. It appears on the back of cereal boxes, it is pictured on posters hung in doctors' offices, and it is taught in our schools. The plate is also supplemented with other recommendations than the ones found on the plate. It has comments about switching milk to 1% or skim, eating more whole grains, varying protein choices, and making half of the plate dedicated to fruits and vegetables.

Recently, however, faculty members at the Harvard School of Public Health decided to take a closer look at the USDA's MyPlate, and the researchers concluded that the USDA's Plate was seriously flawed. They felt the plate did not have the exact right amounts for each of the food groups. In response to this, Harvard released their own version of MyPlate, calling it the Harvard Healthy Eating Plate. On their plate, Harvard made it so that there was a higher vegetable to fruit ratio than was found on MyPlate. Harvard also added healthy oils and water to their plate, stating that dairy should be consumed sparingly. Furthermore, the Harvard study concluded that the USDA's Pyramid overlooked a basic fact: Even if a person ate the healthiest diet possible, if that person did not exercise he would still not be healthy. Harvard added a section on exercising to their plate due to this. The difference between these plates highlights one reason Americans may be having difficulty controlling their weight: They are confused and misinformed about what and how much they should eat.

The problem of Americans' confusion over what constitutes a healthy diet is complicated by changes in our eating habits over the decades. Many people have become increasingly reliant on the high-fat, high-Calorie foods, and less reliant on the whole grains, vegetables, fruits, high-**fiber** foods, and healthy oils that make up the bulk of Harvard's plate. Why? Three main reasons: convenience, cost, and taste. Many people juggling work, family, and additional commitments find that fast and prepackaged foods are often the only way to get supper on the table. The problem is that these types of foods are almost always higher in fat, salt, sugar, and empty Calories than foods made from scratch. Cost is another factor. Many of these foods (foods like pasta and potatoes) are not only easy to prepare and filling, they are also very affordable. Many foods, like whole-grain products and fresh vegetables and fruits, are much more expensive. And then there is the matter of taste. Those high-fat, high-Calorie foods may not be as healthy as whole grains, vegetables, and fruits, but they taste oh so good. Yes, a carrot or an apple tastes good too, but for some reason, they just never seem irresistible or wholly satisfying the way a bag of greasy, salty potato chips seems.

Convenience, cost, and taste may not be the only things driving us to choose unhealthy foods over healthy ones. Some researchers theorize that our eating habits are driven by millennia of evolution. According to such theories, human beings may actually be hardwired to desire fattening foods and to gain weight. If you're like many people, you might have a sweet tooth, love salty foods, and crave fatty and Calorie-rich foods. For many of us, fat, salt, and sugar—the things we should eat the least of—are also the things we crave the most. We humans can't seem to resist the stuff! But why would your body desire foods that you don't need and that can even be unhealthy for you?

As Daniel E. Lieberman, an op-ed contributor for the *New York Times*, reported in a 2012 article, human beings evolved to crave high-Calorie foods because life was hard for early humans. We had to catch or find all our food, which was extremely time- and energy-consuming. In fact, early humans probably spent nearly every moment of every day searching, chasing after, and fighting for their food. And more food wasn't guaranteed to show up tomorrow. If you had it, you'd better eat it, and as much of it as you could get. Those who ate the most Calories survived, and those who ate the least, well

Not All Bodies Are the Same / 35

. . . they starved to death. It's only within the last century (and in the wealthiest countries) that food has suddenly become so plentiful and easy for most people to obtain. Our evolution, however, occurred over millions of years in which our bodies told us to eat every Calorie-rich food in sight. It's not easy to give up millions of years of craving, so most people still find the fattiest, saltiest, and most sugary foods to also be the tastiest and most desirable.

However, as we previously stated, weight gain isn't just determined by how much energy you take in. It's also determined by how much energy you exert. While Americans have been taking in more Calorie-rich foods, we've been exerting less energy. The traditional exercise requirements cited by doctors are that people should get at least thirty minutes of moderately intense exercise a minimum of three times a week. More recent studies, however, say that these requirements are no longer adequate for the average American. It was always assumed that the half hour three times a week requirement would come on top of additional daily physical activities. But for many people, the increasingly sedentary American lifestyle provides almost no daily activity at all, and if that is the case, half an hour three times a week is not going to be enough to ensure people's health. New recommendations cite one hour of moderately intense activity every day as a minimum for good health, though others state to exercise a minimum of two and a half hours each week.

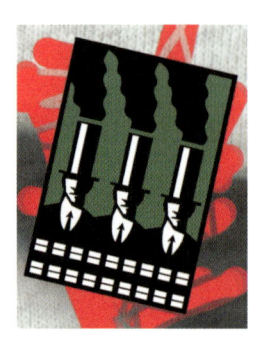

A World of Difference

Even after considering all these issues concerning eating and exercising, there are still other complications to consider in the issue of weight gain, because weight gain or loss isn't just about how much energy you take in or how much energy you burn. It's also about what

Make Connections: Three Body Categories

Generally speaking, doctors classify different body types into three broad categories: ectomorphs, endomorphs, and mesomorphs. People with the ectomorph body type have a lean build, generally do not have a very muscular appearance, and have a naturally speedy metabolism. That person we all know who can eat whatever she wants and never exercises is probably an ectomorph. People with the endomorph body type tend to have a rounder build, a higher proportion of body fat, and a slower metabolism. An endomorph, even if he eats right, exercises, and is very healthy, will probably never look like an ectomorph. His body is just different and will generally reflect this difference in his appearance. Endomorphs, while not being able to necessarily achieve the slimness that ectomorphs can achieve, have an easier time building muscle mass. A person with the mesomorph body type is someone between these extremes.

> **Research Project**
>
> Go to the CDC website to find your BMI (www.cdc.gov/healthyweight/assessing/bmi/childrens_bmi/about_childrens_bmi.html). Now compare your BMI to the ranges that are considered healthy and unhealthy. Where do you fall? Now go online and read about some more of the problems with the BMI system. Are there any famous athletes who might have high BMIs, but are healthy because most of their weight comes from muscle?

type of body you have. The speed at which your body uses energy depends on something called your **metabolism**. Every person's body is different, and different people's bodies have different metabolic rates. We all seem to know someone who can eat and eat and eat, indulge in chips, chocolate, ice cream, and cake, never exercise, and yet never gain an ounce. These lucky individuals have very high metabolic rates, and their bodies burn energy as fast as they can pack in those energy-rich foods. Then there are those of us who seem to just eat an ounce of high-Calorie food and somehow gain a pound. Back in those bygone days when starvation lurked around every corner, those of us with slow metabolisms would have had a much better chance of making it through a hard winter or surviving a famine. Today, a slow metabolism rate is no longer a blessing. It opens the door for weight gain and the health risks and discrimination weight gain can bring.

To a certain degree, metabolism can be adjusted. When you exercise, you increase your metabolism rate, and your body begins to burn energy faster. You can also increase your metabolism by building muscle. Muscle tissue

> **Text-Dependent Questions:**
>
> 1. Why are the thin body types portrayed in magazines and other media unhealthy?
> 2. Why can't you tell how healthy someone is by looking at them?
> 3. What is BMI? What is the equation to find BMI?
> 4. What can the size of your waist, combined with BMI, tell you about your health?
> 5. What happens if you eat more calories than you burn every day?

takes more energy to maintain than fat tissue, so converting fat to muscle causes a corresponding increase in metabolism. A body with more muscle burns more energy even when at rest. However, people naturally have different shapes, sizes, and metabolisms, and although some adjustments can be made through lifestyle and exercise, a person can't simply change her whole body chemistry. Many scientists believe that much about a person's body shape, size, and metabolism is caused by genetics.

People who blame and judge others because of overweight and obesity fail to understand that these conditions are far more complicated than just choosing to eat too much or to exercise too little. Furthermore, even if a person was 100 percent culpable for his overweight or obesity, that still would not justify other people's judgmental attitudes, prejudice, discrimination, or disdain. Having overweight or obesity does not alter a person's ability to be a friend, perform well in school, hold an important job, or give and receive love. Overweight and obesity are medical conditions of the body, not flaws of the personality, mind, or character.

Words to Understand

economic: Relating to finances or money.

Chapter 3

The Poor Get Fat, the Rich Get Thin?

- Who Gains Weight?
- Is Good Health Something You Learn?
- Barriers to Eating Well
- Health Care: A System of Inequality

Who Gains Weight?

Prejudice and discrimination aren't the only forms of inequality associated with overweight and obesity. Once a person has excess weight, he may certainly face these issues. But there is another type of inequality operating in the obesity epidemic, and this inequality regards who develops overweight or obesity in the first place.

Just about any person, if exposed to the right combination of factors, could become overweight or obese. However, Americans aren't all gaining weight at equal rates. Certain groups of people are much more likely to become overweight or obese than other groups. Several studies have shown that members of certain racial or ethnic groups, people with little education, and people who have little money or live in poverty are at a greatly increased risk of experiencing overweight or obesity. All of these factors are related to something called socioeconomic status, and socioeconomic status can have a significant impact on health, including body size.

Socioeconomic status is the position or level a person occupies in society based on social and **economic** factors like education, employment, and wealth. People with lots of wealth, for example, have a high socioeconomic status, while people with little money have a low socioeconomic status. People with a great deal of education tend to be of high socioeconomic status, and people with little education tend to be of a low socioeconomic status. Race and ethnicity are also linked to socioeconomic status because, due to continued systems of inequality, certain racial and ethnic groups are more likely to be poor and less educated than other racial and ethnic groups.

Many studies show a correlation between socioeconomic status and obesity. You can see the results of one of these studies in the table on page 44. This graph is taken from the National Center for Health Statistics study of the connection between obesity and socioeconomic status of children and adolescents from 2005 to 2008.

42 / Discrimination & Prejudice

The Poor Get Fat, the Rich Get Thin? / 43

The following graph is taken from the National Health and Nutrition Examination survey, found on the CDC website.

Figure 1. Prevalence of obesity among children and adolescents aged 2–19 years, by poverty income ratio, sex, and race and ethnicity: United States, 2005–2008

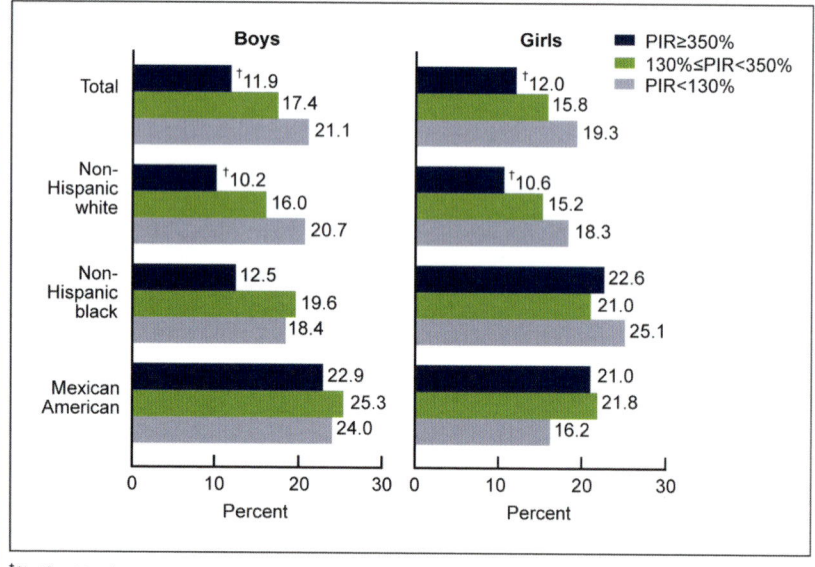

		Boys	Girls
Total	PIR≥350%	†11.9	†12.0
	130%≤PIR<350%	17.4	15.8
	PIR<130%	21.1	19.3
Non-Hispanic white	PIR≥350%	†10.2	†10.6
	130%≤PIR<350%	16.0	15.2
	PIR<130%	20.7	18.3
Non-Hispanic black	PIR≥350%	12.5	22.6
	130%≤PIR<350%	19.6	21.0
	PIR<130%	18.4	25.1
Mexican American	PIR≥350%	22.9	21.0
	130%≤PIR<350%	25.3	21.8
	PIR<130%	24.0	16.2

†Significant trend.
NOTES: PIR is poverty income ratio. Persons of other race and ethnicity included in total.
SOURCE: CDC/NCHS, National Health and Nutrition Examination Survey, 2005–2008.

People of low socioeconomic status experience overweight and obesity at greater rates than people of high socioeconomic status. The debate over why this is so is heated and controversial. Although there are as of yet no clear answers for the connection between socioeconomic status and excess weight, a number of factors very likely play a significant role. Among these factors, access to education, access to food, and access to health services are the most important.

Is Good Health Something You Learn?

Every person is born into this world as a clean slate. At birth, you are completely helpless and know nothing. But very quickly you begin to learn, and in just a few years, you are able to feed, clothe, and entertain yourself largely on your own. These may not seem like huge accomplishments, but considering a human being's starting point, the results after just a few years are astounding. Those results, however, are the product of deliberate education. If no one taught you to feed yourself (either directly or through setting an example that you could easily emulate), you would never learn. The same goes for clothing yourself and for the numerous skills required for your functioning and survival. You need to be taught everything you know, and this education begins at home and continues as you are exposed to the larger society.

Education definitely plays a role in good health and seems to play a role in weight. People do not just naturally know what things are healthy or what leads to weight gain. They need to get this information from somewhere, and the more education a person has, the more information she has access to regarding developing and maintaining good health. People with a high level of education experience certain illnesses and health conditions (especially preventable diseases) less often than people with low levels of education. This is because people with more education tend to be better informed about health risks, ways to prevent health problems, and what the body requires to maintain good health. We can better understand how education impacts public health by looking at two common examples: smoking and AIDS.

The Poor Get Fat, the Rich Get Thin? / 45

Obesity Trends* Among U.S. Adults
BRFSS, 2009
(*BMI ≥30, or ~ 30 lbs. overweight for 5' 4" person)

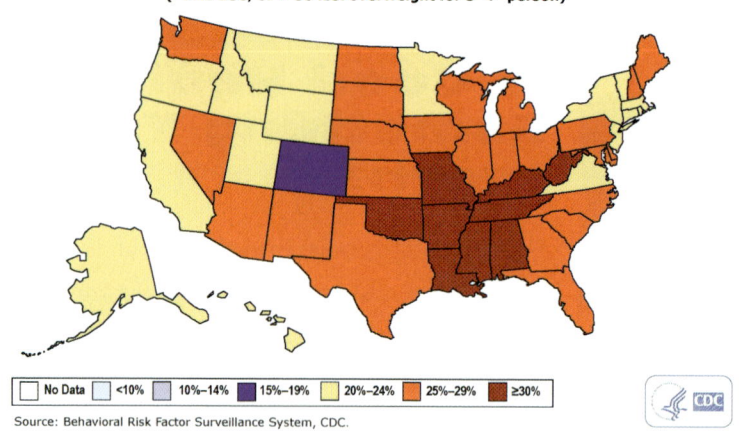

No Data | <10% | 10%–14% | 15%–19% | 20%–24% | 25%–29% | ≥30%

Source: Behavioral Risk Factor Surveillance System, CDC.

Smoking is still relatively common in American society, but compared to a number of decades ago, smoking rates have dropped dramatically. The reason is directly linked to education. Years ago, when practically everyone smoked, few people knew the full health risks associated with the habit. Sure, people knew it wasn't good for them, but for a long time, people honestly did not know that smoking could cause literally hundreds of health complications from numerous forms of cancer, to high blood pressure and heart disease, to osteoporosis and arthritis, to reproductive complications and more. But then both government and private organizations began huge public education campaigns to get the word out about how dangerous smoking really was, and as these campaigns spread, smoking rates dropped. Today, the number of smokers in America is much less than what it used to be because of this education, and our health is better for it.

Another instance in which education made major inroads against a public health crisis is the AIDS epidemic. AIDS is a condition caused by the human immunodeficiency virus (HIV) in which the immune system becomes so weak it can no longer fight off disease. Today we know that HIV is passed from person to person through the exchange of certain body fluids, especially blood and semen. When HIV first began spreading in the United

States, however, no one knew what it was, how it was spread, or how to protect oneself against it. But much like smoking, once people began to understand what HIV was, huge public education campaigns began and transmission rates slowed.

The public education campaigns against smoking and HIV infection have been so large that they have reached people of all socioeconomic groups. Nevertheless, people of lower socioeconomic status (and therefore with less education) continue to smoke at greater rates and be at higher risk for HIV transmission than people of high socioeconomic status. In the case of obesity, public education campaigns are only beginning. The people with the most access to information about obesity and how it can be prevented are people of high socioeconomic status with high education levels. If there is no public education campaign bringing information to you, then you have to go out and get that information on your own. The lower your socioeconomic status, the more difficult this is for you to do. People of high socioeconomic status have much greater access to information sources like health journals, libraries, university resources, the Internet, and various forms of media and

> *In 2012, West Virginia, at 33.5 percent, had the highest obesity rate of any state. Mississippi, Arkansas, Louisiana, and Alabama were close behind with prevalence rates of 32.2, 31.4, 30.9, and 30.4 percent, respectively.*

are therefore more likely to be educated about excess weight, its causes, its health effects, and modes of prevention.

Barriers to Eating Well

Access to food is another factor influenced by socioeconomic status. You might assume that the biggest food-related issue for people of low socioeconomic status is simply getting enough food. For some people this certainly is a major concern, but it is not the factor influencing the relationship between socioeconomic status and obesity. Instead, it is the *types* of food that people of low socioeconomic status have access to that creates the biggest weight-related health risk for this group. In general, people of low socioeconomic status have a more difficult time maintaining a well-balanced, low-fat/low-Calorie diet than people of higher socioeconomic status.

There are a number of reasons for the inequity in diet between socioeconomic groups, but cost is definitely one of the biggest. Unfortunately, in America today, some of the healthiest foods are also some of the most expensive. Foods like whole-grain breads and cereals, fresh vegetables and fruits, and healthy oils are very nutritious, but they can also be very costly. If your grocery budget needs to really stretch, you are more likely to spend your money on high-volume, low-cost, nonperishable foods. Unfortunately, many of these foods are also low in nutritional value and high in empty Calories.

The problem of access to nutritious food is often compounded by where a person lives. High-end grocery stores, the type that sell a wide variety of fresh produce, whole-grain foods, and health foods, tend to be located in high-income areas. This makes sense to companies; since they are selling high-cost products, why would they put their stores in areas where the people can't afford to purchase the goods? Low-end grocery stores, those that sell lots of high-bulk, high-Calorie foods but little fresh produce or health

food, tend to be located in lower-income areas. This creates a serious problem for people living in these areas. Even if they wanted to spend a little extra to buy some healthier groceries, they simply might not have access to those healthy products. Furthermore, unlike people of high socioeconomic status who have cars and can easily drive themselves to the best grocery stores, many people of low socioeconomic status have no cars and must rely on public transportation. If you can't afford that transportation, or if the transportation service doesn't go to a high-end grocery store, you're stuck with the food you can buy within walking distance of your home.

The situation of access to healthy food seems even more unfair when one realizes that not all these conditions have to be this way. Some foods are more expensive for legitimate reasons. For example, the cost of fresh produce in grocery stores in city centers is often much higher than the cost of produce in grocery stores in other areas. One of the reasons is that it can cost more for transportation to get the fresh produce to that city grocery store. This increase in transportation costs leads to an increase in price for the consumer. But not all healthy foods need to be as expensive as they are. In image-conscious America, however, many companies have realized that they can make a lot of money on healthy foods. People who can afford to often spend much more for foods that will help maintain good health and keep weight down, and some companies put huge markups on the price of health foods—whether or not these foods actually cost more

50 / Discrimination & Prejudice

to produce or transport. In America, healthy food has in some cases become a luxury item because companies realize that labels like "healthy," "organic," "all-natural," and "low-fat" have become sought-after commodities. All too often, these are luxury items that people of low socioeconomic status simply can't afford.

Health Care: A System of Inequality

Access to education and access to healthy food are certainly major factors contributing to excess weight in people of lower socioeconomic status, but perhaps the biggest factor is access to health services. Think about it, when was the last time you saw a well-equipped fitness facility or health spa in a low-income area? If a person is lucky, her area may have a community center with some sports facilities, but the gyms with numerous fitness programs, various machines, and high-tech equipment are playgrounds for the higher classes. Health facilities like these cost a lot of money to build and maintain, have expensive membership rates, and are way out of the price range for most people of low socioeconomic status.

> According to the U.S. Census Bureau, in 2003 approximately 45 million Americans, or 15.6 percent of the population, had no health insurance.

A well-equipped fitness facility, however, certainly isn't a requirement for good health. Yes, one of the major contributors to the obesity crisis is an overall decline in physical activity rates, but you can be physically active just by going outside and taking a walk. That doesn't require a gym membership. People of low socioeconomic status, however, can have limited opportunities to just go outside and take a walk. Low-income areas tend to have fewer public spaces, like well-maintained parks and sidewalks, suitable for these types

> "Obesity itself has become a lifelong disease, not a cosmetic issue, nor a moral judgment."
> —Robert H. Eckel, M.D., Former Vice Chairman of the American Heart Association

of activities. Low-income areas often suffer from higher crime rates as well, making outdoor activities less safe and enjoyable. Furthermore, many people of low socioeconomic status have to work long hours, or even at more than one job, to make ends meet. That leaves little time or energy for exercise.

The biggest contributor to less access to health resources however is inequities in the health-care system. Unlike Canada and many European countries, the United States has no system of guaranteed health care. Some people are eligible for certain state or federal health-care programs, but the majority of people must obtain health insurance coverage either through an employer or by purchasing that coverage themselves. Health insurance is expensive, and many people of lower socioeconomic status simply can't afford it.

It isn't just health insurance that is expensive, however. Health care itself is incredibly pricy. In many areas of the country, even a routine doctor's visit can cost more than fifty dollars. Just a few blood tests can cost hundreds of dollars. One trip to the emergency room can cost thousands of dollars. Few people in the United States can afford to pay for regular routine medical care let alone for a big hospital bill on their own. If you don't have health insurance to help cover these costs, you are less likely to seek medical care, even if you really need it. This puts people of lower socioeconomic status at greater risk both for developing health problems and for experiencing more severe

> **Research Project**
>
> In 2010, the United States passed a new law known as the Affordable Care Act, which introduced new requirements for how insurance companies deal with obesity. Go online and find out the details. Under the new law, will more or fewer people have coverage for obesity and overweight?

consequences from those health problems than they would experience if they had greater access to medical care.

Why would lack of health insurance or lack of access to health care affect excess weight and obesity? As we have already discussed, many people believe that overweight and obesity are personal issues over which individuals exercise control (or lack of control). More and more, however, we are coming to understand that overweight and obesity are in fact medical conditions and need to be treated in the same way other medical conditions and diseases are treated: with the care, advice, and expertise of doctors. With appropriate medical care, obesity is easier to prevent and easier to treat. Studies have shown that if left to deal with obesity on their own, individuals are almost guaranteed to fail to bring their weight down to a healthy level. Could you treat a condition like heart disease or epilepsy on your own without appropriate medical care? Of course not. Similarly, a person with obesity needs the help of a medical professional to manage the condition appropriately. People of low socioeconomic status have a much more difficult time accessing this help than do people of a high socioeconomic status.

Even if a person has health insurance to help cover medical expenses, however, he is still not guaranteed medical help for weight-related issues.

> **Text-Dependent Questions:**
>
> 1. Why are certain demographic groups more likely to be overweight or obese?
> 2. What are two factors that may explain the connection between socioeconomic status and rates of overweight and obesity?
> 3. How was education responsible for reducing smoking rates in the United States?
> 4. Why might grocery stores with expensive, healthy food not be found as often in low-income areas?
> 5. What are some health care facilities that those in lower socioeconomic classes might not have access to?

Many health insurance plans specifically exclude coverage for treatments of weight-related conditions. So, even if your doctor prescribes a weight-loss medication, weight-related surgery, or some other weight-loss program, your health insurance company can refuse to pay. This denial of coverage may be discriminatory, but it is not illegal. The idea that overweight and obesity are personal rather than medical problems is still so prevalent that health insurance companies can deny coverage. To make matters even worse, many doctors still do not recognize overweight and obesity as legitimate medical conditions and therefore fail to properly treat them. A person with overweight or obesity can still walk into a doctor's office for a checkup and walk right back out twenty minutes later without the issue of weight ever being addressed. Thankfully, attitudes in the medical profession are definitely changing, and more and more doctors are seeing themselves as having a larger responsibility toward their patients who are experiencing excess weight. But many outdated attitudes still persist.

Words to Understand

consumer culture: The beliefs and values that influence spending and consumption patterns.
savvy: Shrewdness and practical knowledge.
malleable: Easily influenced or persuaded by others.
exploit: To take advantage of in a negative way.
disposable income: Money that is left over after bills are paid.
stipulate: Specify.
quotas: Proportional shares of something that one should contribute or receive.

Chapter 4

Big Targets: Advertising and America's Obesity Epidemic

- Personally Responsible or Driven to Eat?
- Get Them While They're Young
- Captive Audience

Personally Responsible or Driven to Eat?

Socioeconomic status is far from the only factor that puts a person at risk for gaining excess weight. As we've already stated, numerous changes in the American lifestyle are contributing to the obesity epidemic, and many of these changes affect all of us, no matter what our socioeconomic status and no matter what our body size.

America's **consumer culture** is definitely contributing to rising obesity rates, and the strongest force driving that consumer culture is advertising. Some of the most powerful and **savvy** advertisers are food companies selling unhealthy products that contribute to weight gain. It's easy for many people to claim that what we eat (and any resulting weight gain) is a matter of personal choice, but in America today, the food industry spends billions of dollars and has an army of highly skilled people working to influence the choices we make about what we eat. And the kings of unhealthy food—the fast-food, beverage, and snack manufacturers—are also the ultimate masters of manipulation in the advertising world. Many of today's most successful advertising tactics were developed by fast-food giants. Today, there are thousands upon thousands of fast-food restaurants across the United States. In fact, you can drive through sections of many towns and find a fast-food restaurant on every corner. This means stiff competition. The best tool the fast-food industry has to get your business is advertising. When it comes to advertising, fast-food restaurants pull no punches. They spend billions of dollars every year trying to convince you that their food is irresistible. When they succeed, our waistlines often suffer.

Over the years, advertising has changed in an important way. It used to be almost solely directed at adults. The reason was quite logical. Adults have the jobs, and adults have the money, so messages about where to spend that money should be aimed at those adults. But fast-food companies realized something early on. Children usually have more influence with their parents than companies have. If a fast-food company could get children to want a product, those children would go to their parents, beg and plead, and often be successful in getting what they wanted. When an advertisement aimed at an adult was successful, it might bring in one customer. When an advertisement aimed at a child was successful, it often brought in three or more customers (the child and the child's parents and siblings). Marketing to children, of course, is in no way limited to the fast-food industry. Today all kinds of manufacturers, from those who make toys to those who make cars, realize that the best way to get into Mom or Dad's pocket is through Child. Kids mean big money.

Get Them While They're Young

Companies that advertised to children learned another important lesson: a child converted will be a customer for life. Companies believed that if they could get a child to become loyal to their brand and products early on, that child would remain loyal for the rest of his life. A

Big Targets: Advertising and America's Obesity Epidemic / 59

child who started eating McDonald's before he tasted Burger King, the theory went, would continue eating McDonald's. A child who started drinking Coke before she tasted Pepsi would always prefer Coke. A person who had pleasant memories of slurping milk shakes as a child would slurp milk shakes as an adult. The companies were right. Brand loyalty, a person's commitment to a specific brand, often has less to do with the actual quality of the product than with how early and successfully the brand can be etched into the person's consciousness.

That most famous of the fast-food giants, McDonald's, was the first and for a long time remained the leader in the industry's advertising to children. Ronald McDonald, Hamburgler, and other characters appeared frequently during children's television programming. McDonaldlands and Playlands promised safe and wholesome fun for children, and Happy Meals complete with toys promised . . . well . . . happiness to kids. McDonald's may have led the trend, but everyone else quickly caught on. The messages also became more varied. Soon advertisements aimed at parents portrayed bringing your kids to a fast-food restaurant as a sign of good parenting, a way to make up for spending so much time at work and away from the family, and a way to increase children's love and affection. Advertisements to children stressed the benefits for their parents—the food would be tasty, quick, and affordable—thereby arming the kids with "nag-ammunition." The advertisements basically coach kids on what to say to convince their parents that going out for fast food is a good idea. These forms of advertising are by no means limited to the fast food sold in restaurants. They are used to sell the packaged foods in vending machines and grocery stores as well. In November of 2006, a program called the Children's Food and Beverage Advertising Initiative (CFBAI) was introduced. This goal of this initiative was to shift child-directed advertising away from unhealthy foods. Currently, there are 17 participants of this initiative. However, according to a study done in 2013, children are still seeing a large amount of food ads despite the CFBAI standards and goals.

Today, all kinds of people are employed in the business of marketing to children, and they use numerous tools to figure out how best to influence their **malleable** minds and emotions. Psychiatrists give analyses of children's dreams. Researchers explore the effects of bright colors on the child

62 / *Discrimination & Prejudice*

> "The challenge of the campaign is to make customers believe that McDonald's is their 'Trusted Friend.'"
> —Ray Bergold, McDonald's top marketing executive

brain. Artists and designers develop eye-catching logos and child-friendly characters. Young children are largely powerless against this onslaught. Studies have shown that young children can't distinguish between regular television entertainment and commercials. They don't know that they are being seduced by advertising and that their minds, emotions, and desires are being carefully manipulated by people with huge amounts of money, research, and expertise. They also don't yet have the skills to determine if advertising claims are trustworthy or not. If you tell a young child that a candy bar will make her strong, for example, she will believe you. Children are defenseless against advertising, and fast-food corporations know it. According to James McNeal, author of *Kids as Customers* and *The Kids' Market: Myths and Realities*, companies begin influencing children when they are as young as two years old. By the time they are three years old, many children can recognize brand logos. Furthermore, exhausted parents may often feel defenseless against children's constant nagging. Fast-food corporations know this too and put lots of research money into finding the best way to **exploit** what they call the "nag factor."

Young children aren't the only ones being targeted by advertising. In the last twenty years, teens have emerged as a huge market force. Besides money received as allowances or gifts, many teens work. Today's teens have more

64 / *Discrimination & Prejudice*

disposable income than they ever had before. Each year, spending on purchases by teens or for teens reaches $208.7 billion. That's a huge amount of money, and fast-food companies want their share. To make sure they are getting as much of young people's money as possible, food and drink corporations have embarked on a huge and disturbing trend. They've moved into your schools.

Captive Audience

Many American schools have faced serious financial difficulties in recent decades. Cuts in government spending, opposition to tax increases, and increasing enrollments have left some schools gasping for funds. When food and soft drink manufacturers began offering thousands of dollars for the privilege of getting their products and advertisements into the schools, many districts

Make Connections: Fast Food in Schools

At the same time that schools are opening their doors to the fast-food and beverage industries, they are being forced to eliminate healthy programs like recess and physical education. Even in school some young people now have greater access to unhealthy foods than they have to exercise.

Big Targets: Advertising and America's Obesity Epidemic / 65

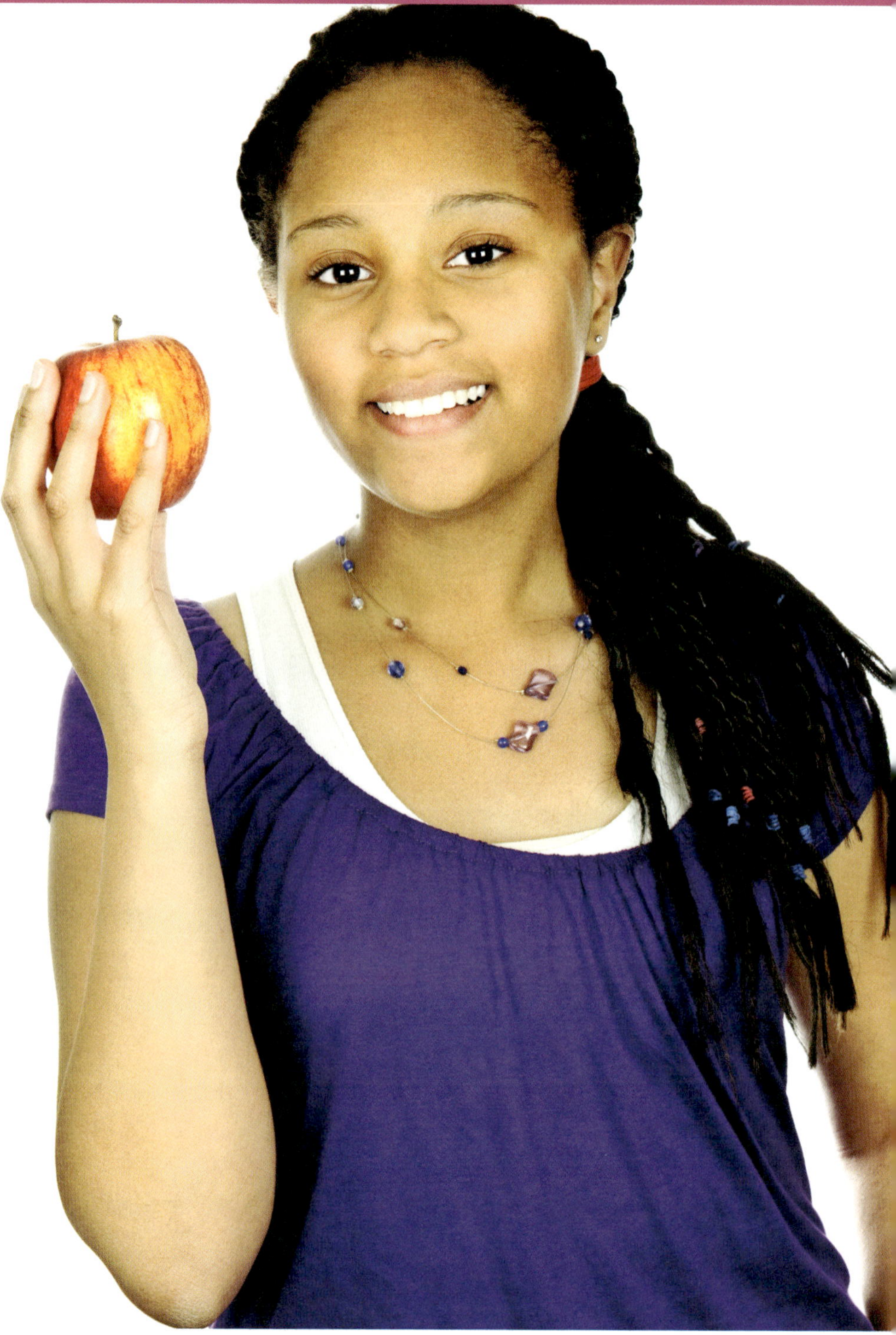

> ## Research Project
>
> Fast-food companies advertise in schools in more ways than one. Go online and see if you can find out more about the topic. What are some ways that fast-food companies advertise through funding school programs? What about sports? Do you think this is good or bad?

rushed to sign up. Advertising on television and in print was good, but young people still had the power to turn off the TV or put down the magazine. Furthermore, if they're not on summer vacation, young people are spending most of each day at school where they can't watch television or read magazines. If food and beverage companies could get into the schools, they could not only reach children and teens during this otherwise inaccessible part of the day, the companies could have them as a captive audience. After all, you can't just walk out of a school because you don't want to see an advertisement.

Today food and beverage companies not only have their vending machines in the hallways, advertisements on the walls, billboards on school buses, and logos plastered at sports events. They have also taken over many school lunch programs. America's government-sponsored school lunch program was never completely healthy to begin with, but today it has definitely taken a turn for the worse. For many schools, gone are the days of a sloppy joe, mashed potatoes, an apple, and a carton of milk. Today, many children and teens go to the school cafeteria to grab pizza, cheeseburgers, chips, Coke, Pepsi, and fries. Depending on their contracts, schools may even get a percentage of the fast-food or beverage sales. Worse yet, some schools have contracts that **stipulate** minimum sales **quotas**; if those quotas aren't met, the school can lose some of the promised revenues. This has led to some schools allowing soft drinks and snacks to be purchased in the hallways and consumed in the classrooms. The need for money to support their programs has turned some schools into accomplices of the food and beverage industries.

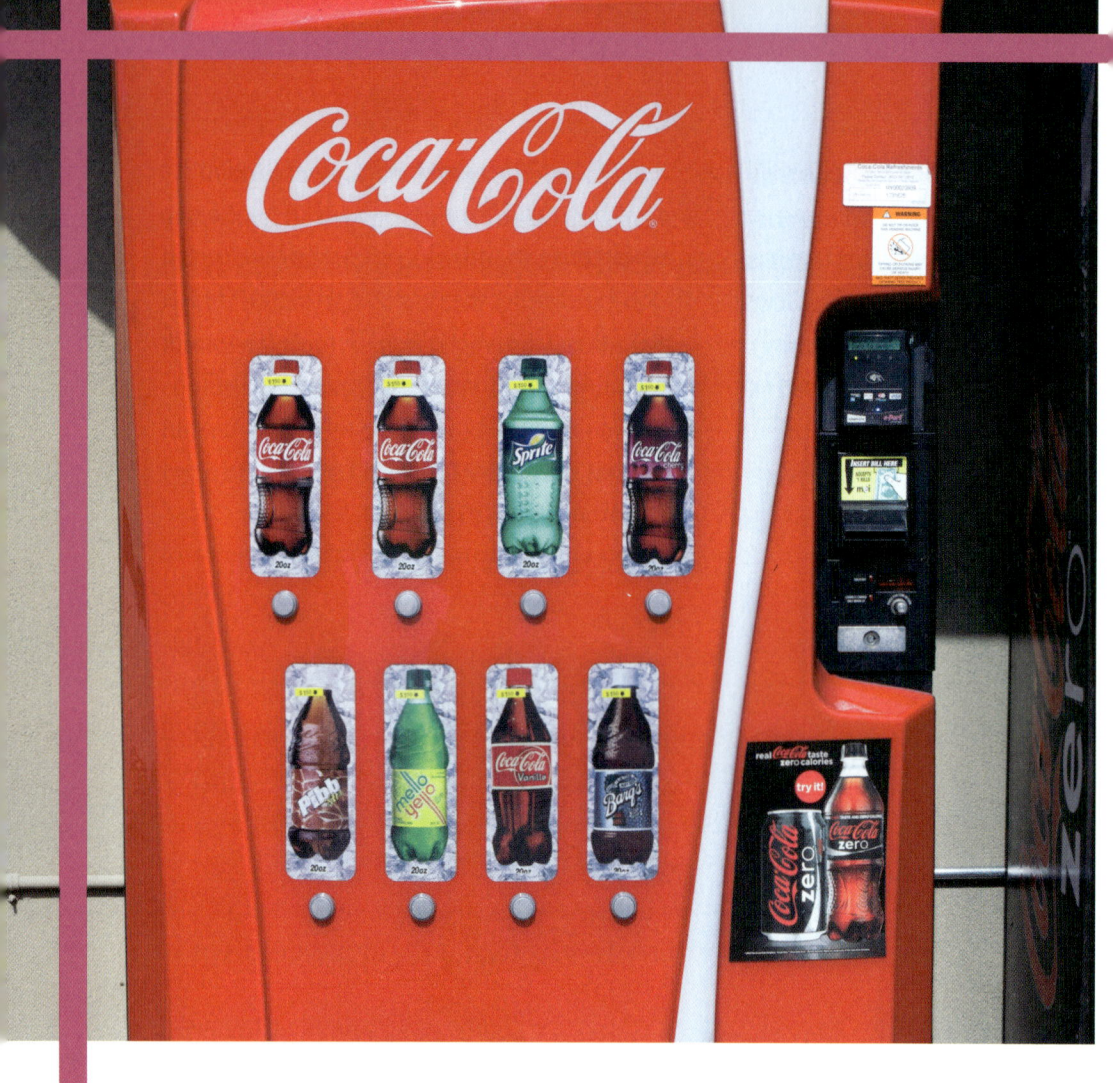

Some schools now work with these industries to encourage fast-food consumption and maximize sales. And here socioeconomic status becomes a risk factor again. Schools in low-income areas have less funding and may therefore become more reliant on deals with food corporations than the

> **Text-Dependent Questions:**
>
> 1. Why do fast-food companies spend so much money on advertising?
> 2. Why do companies target children with their advertising?
> 3. What is the "nag factor?"
> 4. Why have some schools agreed to sell fast food in their buildings?
> 5. Why are poorer schools more likely to agree to enter into contracts with fast-food companies?

better-funded schools in high-income areas. Once again, socioeconomic inequalities put certain populations at greater risk for developing obesity.

The presence of fast foods in schools undermines parents' ability to make healthy food choices for their children. More than that, it gives fast-food and beverage companies easy access to young people whose eating habits and lifestyles are still developing. Studies show that the habits we form when we are young usually stay with us for life and are the most difficult to break. A person who starts smoking at a young age will fight a difficult battle if she wants to quit and may very well end up smoking for life. Similarly, a person who starts eating fast food and drinking sugary soft drinks on a regular basis early on will carry those eating habits into adulthood and may end up fighting a lifelong battle against obesity. We can be quick to blame people with overweight and obesity, but more and more children barely have a fighting chance against the powerful forces contributing to the crisis.

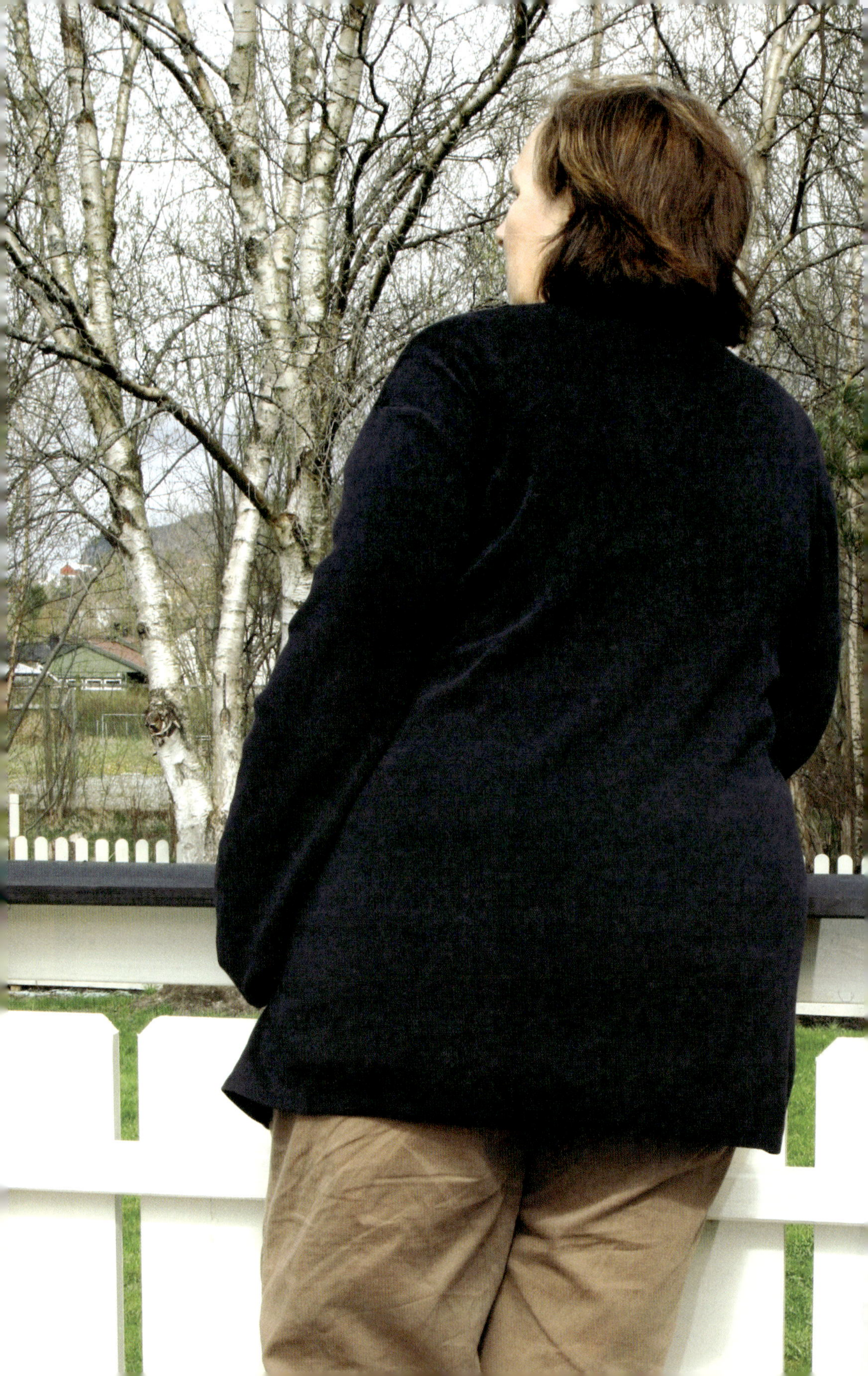

chapter 5

Life Is Different if You're "Fat"

- Social Pariah

- A Stifled Future

- Denied the Job

72 / Discrimination & Prejudice

No matter what background a person comes from or why her excess weight developed, once she has overweight or obesity, she will face many challenges. Now that you have a better understanding of what overweight and obesity are, some of the factors that contribute to overweight and obesity, and who is most at risk for these conditions, let's take a closer look at the most common forms of weight discrimination. Overt discrimination against people with excess weight is most common in three specific areas: social interaction, education, and employment.

Social Pariah

It probably comes as no surprise that people with excess weight face discrimination in social interactions. After all, we've all heard people yell insults like "fatso" or "thunder thighs." We've all heard (and maybe even laughed at) fat jokes. And we're all familiar with the story of the "nicest guy in the world" who is always denied a date because "there's just no spark." For a person with overweight or obesity, these situations usually aren't isolated incidents. They happen every day and can add up to a lifetime of misery.

A number of studies support the assertion that social discrimination is more than just the occasional unkind remark or judgmental comment. In 1961, a study was done that became famous. In the study, which was reported in the *American Sociological Review*, researchers asked children to rank a group of photographs according to which person they would most like to be friends with. The photographs depicted children with different physical characteristics and included a child in a wheelchair, a child with an amputated hand, a child with a facial disfigurement, a child who was overweight, and others. The majority of the study's participants ranked the overweight child as the person with whom they would least want to be friends. In 2000 and 2001, forty years after the original study, Janet Latner of Rutgers University and Albert Stunkard of the University of Pennsylvania decided to repeat the study. Their results were even more dramatic, and in *Stigma and Childhood Obesity: Forty Years Later*, they conclude that children's negative perceptions of people with overweight and obesity are even stronger now than they were forty years ago.

Another study published in 2012 examined the relationship between body size and bullying. In this study, researchers surveyed overweight youths between the ages of fourteen and eighteen that were enrolled in two national weight loss camps. When asked if they had been the victims of teasing due to body weight (if so, for how long), and who it was that bullied and teased them. The results showed that it was not only peers or strangers that made fun of overweight youth. Sixty-four percent of participants had been bullied at school, 78 percent reported the bullying for one year and 36 percent for five years. The people that were most likely to bully or tease the overweight youth were peers (92 percent), friends (70 percent), physical education teachers or sport coaches (42 percent), parents (37 percent), and teachers (27 percent). The teasing was mostly verbal, but instances of cyberbullying and physical aggression were also recounted. Among those studied, it was clear that body size significantly impacted social interaction.

"For fat students, the school experience is one of ongoing prejudice, unnoticed discrimination, and almost constant harassment. . . . From nursery school through college, fat students experience ostracism, discouragement, and sometimes violence."
—National Education Association, "Report on Discrimination Due to Physical Size," 1994.

76 / Discrimination & Prejudice

A Stifled Future

Social interactions in the school environment are often the first place young people are exposed to weight discrimination. However, weight discrimination in the school environment exists in another form as well. Studies also show that people who are overweight or obese have lower levels of educational attainment than people of medically "normal" weights. But, contrary to some long-held, prejudiced opinions, this isn't because people with excess weight are any less intelligent or capable than their "normal" weight peers. It's because other people and systems erect barriers to their success.

One barrier to educational attainment is low self-esteem. People with excess weight suffer from low self-esteem at much higher rates than people of "normal" weight. A new study of 6,500 participants in Britain found that children with low self-esteem tend to be heavier as adults, gaining weight over twenty years. Other studies have found that low self-esteem is a result of obesity. Either way, it is clear that obesity and low self-esteem are in some way connected, and both can have a strong impact on an overweight child. When a child is exposed to constant feelings of shame and begins to see himself as in some way responsible for bullying or lack of friends, his self-esteem suffers. People with low self-esteem have a more difficult time achieving difficult goals or taking risks. If a person does not believe in herself and her abilities, she is less likely to attempt or even to consider higher aspirations. People with low self-esteem often end up settling for the low aspirations and expectations defined for them by others. Low self-esteem can become a significant barrier to educational success.

Low expectations for people with overweight and obesity abound. This is regularly enforced by the media according to Rebecca Puhl, a Yale researcher. Puhl looked at and analyzed 370 news videos that could be found on the websites of major networks. From these videos, Puhl found that adults who were obese or overweight were negatively depicted 65 percent of the time, and obese children were portrayed negatively 77 percent of the time. Puhl stated, "[The news videos] have a very unflattering emphasis on body parts like stomach or buttocks, or else they show them eating unhealthy food, exhibiting sedentary behavior, and wearing ill-fitting clothes." It is difficult to combat stereotypes when the media is enforcing this negative view. This lack of financial support can make it not only more difficult for overweight students to complete higher education, but discourage them from pursuing higher education in the first place.

For most people, higher education opens doors to good jobs and a better future. For people struggling with overweight and obesity, however, successful completion of higher education won't necessarily guarantee successful employment. They can quickly learn that weight discrimination doesn't suddenly end at the school gates. It follows people into the working world.

Denied the Job

In October 2004, Misty Watts' experience of weight discrimination became national news when her story appeared on ABC News. Watts, a part-time college student and mother of three, had worked at Ruby Tuesday, a national restaurant chain, for two years. She was apparently good at her job, as evidenced by being awarded Employee of the Month just days before a summons from her district manager. He was not summoning Watts to congratulate her. He was firing her. Her district manager's reason was simple and direct. Watts' uniform did not fit properly, and she would not be able to buy one that would fit properly. Although he did not say it, the reason Watts' uniform did not fit was because of her weight, and the reason she could not buy one that would fit was because they did not make uniforms large enough for Watts' size.

When Watts' story became national news, Ruby Tuesday denied that it terminates employees because of weight, but they did not deny that appearance was an important criterion for employment with the company. In a written statement to ABC News, the company stated, "We want our team members . . . to wear . . . shirts, blouses, and jeans that fit properly . . . our people are the point of direct contact with all our guests. That is why it is so

Life Is Different if You're "Fat" / 79

important for us to have team members who look and perform their best . . . ." As the story gained more attention, however, the company apparently changed its opinion about Misty Watts' appearance and performance; they offered Watts her job back. She had had enough, though, and turned it down.

Misty Watts' experience is not that unusual. Employment is another area in which weight discrimination is prevalent, and anecdotal accounts like Watts' aren't the only evidence. Numerous studies also support this claim. In a 2012 study published in the *International Journal of Obesity* researched this employment discrimination. For this study, researchers gave participants a number of resumes that had pictures of applicants both before and after they had weight-loss surgery. What they discovered was that there were disparities between starting salaries, supposed leadership potential, and the selection of the candidate for the occupation. This study only looked at women, but it has been found in other studies that while overweight men do not face the same type of discrimination in the workplace as overweight women, extremely obese men do have lower salaries and less chances of receiving promotions. Another study found that discrimination based on weight had a more profound effect in hiring practices than discrimination based on gender.

Maryanne Bodolay of the National Association to Advance Fat Acceptance (NAAFA) says inequality affects employment long before the first paycheck is received. In fact, one of the most common places weight discrimination is experienced is in the hiring process. According to Bodolay, qualified workers who happen to be overweight or obese may have no problem landing an interview, but are often stopped short the minute potential employers meet them face to face. Their resumes may be impeccable, but often employers feel that overweight and obese people just don't look the part. In too many cases, "the look" becomes more important than the skills.

One of the reasons people with excess weight have trouble "looking the part" for the corporate world is quite simple—they can't get the "right" clothes. Image isn't just important in the media and popular culture. Image

> **Michigan is the only state where it is illegal to discriminate on the basis of weight. Similarly, San Francisco and Santa Cruz (California), Urbana (Illinois), Madison (Wisconsin), Birmingham (New York), and Washington, D.C., are the only American cities with local laws against weight discrimination.**

is also seen as extremely important in business. Those "power suits" and red ties are supposed to communicate confidence, competence, and strength. In the business world, the saying, "The clothes make the man," still applies to a surprising degree (to women as well as to men). Few clothing manufacturers, however, make "power" business attire for large people. Large people in need of professional clothes often must go to specialty stores or even have their clothing custom made—an extremely costly endeavor—often too costly for the person who hasn't yet landed the job. An inability to find appropriate clothes may not seem very significant, but it can have a big impact on a person's life. Furthermore it is just one aspect of yet another larger issue of weight discrimination: lack of access to products and services.

The inability to find and afford appropriate formal and business attire is just one example of how people with overweight and obesity experience inequality in their access to goods and services. From finding comfortable furniture, to using the narrow stalls of public restrooms, to being forced to purchase two tickets when traveling on buses or aircraft, people with excess

Make Connections: Working for Change

Discrimination against people with excess weight is a reality in America, but it doesn't have to hold a person back. There are many people in America today who have succeeded in spite of facing discrimination and use their success to fight against inequality. Actor Camryn Manheim is just one of these individuals. Manheim has won numerous awards for her work in television, theater, and film, including an Emmy and a Golden Globe Award. Manheim, however, has much more than awards to be proud of. Before becoming a famous actor, she worked as a sign-language interpreter in hospital delivery rooms. She continues to work for people with deafness and disabilities, and she is a board member of the American Civil Liberties Union. She is also the author of a *New York Times* best-selling book, *Wake Up, I'm Fat!*

weight can experience many frustrations in daily life, and the larger one's body, the larger these frustrations will be. Many people argue that lack of access to products and services may be an inconvenience, but it does not constitute discrimination. They may be correct, but the situation is just one more example of how people of "normal weight" set standards that make life more difficult for people with overweight and obesity. However, products

> **Research Project**
>
> This chapter talked about how certain clothes and other products are not available for people who are overweight or obese. What are some other products that you can think of that fit this description? How could they be changed so they were more suited to a wider range of people? Do you think such changes should be made? Why or why not?

and services are one realm in which American attitudes toward excess weight are beginning to change. As Americans grow larger, more and more companies are realizing that to be competitive they need to offer equal-quality goods and services to people of larger sizes.

> **Text-Dependent Questions:**
>
> 1. What condition do children discriminate against the most?
> 2. How does decreased self-esteem affect educational achievement?
> 3. Who was Misty Watts? Why was she fired from her job?
> 4. Why are clothes important in a work environment?
> 5. How does the lack of access to goods and services affect the lives of the obese and overweight?

Words to Understand

perpetuating: Making something last.

Chapter 6

No Easy Answers

- An Industry Built on Suffering

- The Surgeon General's Call to Action

- Change Your Body or Change Your Attitude?

An Industry Built on Suffering

Excess weight and the social discrimination that results may mean great suffering for some people, but for others it means big business. While new trends in product creation and services are in some cases making people's lives easier, in other cases companies are targeting people of excess weight in an attempt to dupe them into purchasing worthless products. These companies are exploiting for profit people's excess weight and desperation to overcome that weight. Once people are overweight, they become the targets of countless companies selling empty dreams and promises for thinness and acceptance. And who are these companies? Most of them are members of America's huge diet and image industries.

For years people believed that the answer to excess weight was diet and exercise. If you need to lose a few pounds, go on a diet. It sounds so easy, but clearly it's not or the obesity epidemic would not have grown to its current crisis proportions. Whether truly suffering from a weight problem or just believing they would look better if they lost weight, Americans spend billions of their hard-earned dollars every year searching for weight-loss solutions. Prepackaged weight-loss meals, diet shakes, diet soda, sugar-free foods, books, magazines, program memberships, "miracle" drugs, weight-loss machines, "fat-burning" creams—we stand in line and dutifully open our wallets for all these products and more.

But, one might ask, is there anything inherently wrong with the diet industry? After all, overweight and obesity (whether or not you care about conforming to certain beauty standards) are serious health problems with serious consequences. Discrimination against people with overweight and obesity is certainly wrong, but shouldn't people for the sake of their health be motivated to lose weight? If someone has a product that could alleviate these problems, why shouldn't that person or company make the product available to the public and make a profit as well? If the diet industry can improve people's health, how can it possibly be a bad thing?

Certainly excess weight does bring serious health risks, and all people, regardless of their size, should make good (or at least better) health a top priority. But here's the key: much of the diet industry is not built on improving health; it's built on selling an image. And the products it sells are not avenues to success. For the billions of dollars Americans are spending each year, nearly no one is losing weight and keeping it off long term. The truth is Americans don't have an ounce of weight loss to show for all those billions of dollars spent on weight-loss products. The obesity epidemic is still growing. Sadly, the overwhelming majority of the diet industry is not part of the solution; it's part of the problem. The diet industry's mere existence proves that diets do not work. Studies show that people that attempt diets usually gain all of the weight back and more within a couple of years. In fact, the act of dieting increases your body's tendency to gain weight.

So how can the diet industry survive and even grow by leaps and bounds? Because there's a catch: Time. Within five years, two-thirds of dieters regain

No Easy Answers / 87

88 / Discrimination & Prejudice

all the weight they lost (and most gain back even more). In the short term, however, just about any diet can cause a brief, minimal weight loss. Even if all that is lost is water and no fat is truly burned, a quick drop of five or ten pounds can be enough hope to keep a desperate dieter coming back for more. These temporary, rapid weight losses followed by the inevitable weight gain lead to a cycle called "yo-yo" dieting. It's on this that the diet industry survives and thrives. And the more social discrimination people with excess weight face, the more desperate they become to lose weight. So, they return to products that contain little but empty promises again and again.

The Surgeon General's Call to Action

Diets as we have come to know them are certainly not the answer to America's obesity epidemic. Furthermore, as long as we remain so focused on image, it will be difficult to fight the discrimination that affects so many people with excess weight. But this does not mean that there is nothing we can do. In what is called the Surgeon General's Call to Action to Prevent and Decrease Overweight and Obesity, the United States Department of Health and Human Services listed fifteen points of action as national priorities for everyone from individuals, to schools, to the government:

1. Change the perception of overweight and obesity at all ages. The primary concern should be one of health and not appearance.

2. Educate all expectant parents about the many benefits of breast-feeding. Breast-fed infants may be less likely to become overweight as they grow older, and mothers who breast-feed may return to pre-pregnancy weight more quickly.

3. Educate health-care providers and health profession students in the prevention and treatment of overweight and obesity across the life span.

4. Provide culturally appropriate education in schools and communities about healthy eating habits and regular physical activity, based on the *Dietary Guidelines for Americans*, for people of all ages. Emphasize the consumer's role in making wise food and physical activity choices.

5. Ensure daily, quality physical education in all school grades. Such education can develop the knowledge, attitudes, skills, behaviors, and confidence needed to be physically active for life.

6. Reduce time spent watching television and in other similar sedentary behaviors.

7. Build physical activity into regular routines and playtime for children and their families. Ensure that adults get at least thirty minutes of moderate physical activity on most days of the week. Children should aim for at least sixty minutes.

8. Create more opportunities for physical activity at work sites. Encourage all employers to make facilities and opportunities available for physical activity for all employees.

9. Make community facilities available and accessible for physical activity for all people, including the elderly.

10. Promote healthier food choices, including at least four and a half cups of fruits and vegetables each day, and reasonable portion sizes at home, in schools, at work sites, and in communities.

11. Ensure that schools provide healthful foods and beverages on school campuses and at school events by: enforcing existing U.S.

No Easy Answers / 91

Department of Agriculture regulations that prohibit serving foods of minimal nutritional value during mealtimes in school food-service areas, including in vending machines; adopting policies specifying that all foods and beverages available at school contribute toward eating patterns that are consistent with the Dietary Guidelines for Americans; providing more food options that are low in fat, calories, and added sugars such as fruits, vegetables, whole grains, and low-fat or nonfat dairy foods; and reducing access to foods high in fat, calories, and added sugars and to excessive portion sizes.

12. Create mechanisms for appropriate reimbursement for the prevention and treatment of overweight and obesity.

> "Overweight and obesity are among the most pressing new health challenges we face today. Our modern environment has allowed these conditions to increase at alarming rates and become a growing health problem for our nation. By confronting these conditions, we have tremendous opportunities to prevent the unnecessary disease and disability they portend for our future."
> —Tommy G. Thompson, Former Secretary of Health and Human Services

13. Increase research on behavioral and environmental causes of overweight and obesity.

14. Increase research and evaluation on prevention and treatment interventions for overweight and obesity, and develop and disseminate best practice guidelines.

15. Increase research on disparities in the prevalence of overweight and obesity among racial and ethnic, gender, socioeconomic, and age groups; and use this research to identify effective and culturally appropriate interventions.

Change Your Body or Change Your Attitude?

What do you think would happen if all the billions of dollars invested in things like diet shakes and "fat-burning" creams were invested in something else—say in health care for people who can't afford it, in research into the causes of and new treatments for obesity, or into public education campaigns about excess weight, health, and discrimination? What do you think would happen if, instead of people trying to change the way they look, people tried to change the way they think? What would our society be like if people cared more about the way individuals were on the inside than the way they appeared on the outside? What do you think people would consider beautiful if they questioned their assumptions about beauty and searched for it in places other than people's bodies? In America's image-conscious society, the fight against body-hate will not be an easy one, but it is essential that individuals learn to love their own and respect others' bodies if we are to fight the effects of the growing obesity epidemic.

The human body comes in an amazing variety of shapes and sizes. To learn to respect and feel confident in our bodies, no matter what their shape or size, we need to shift our focus from impossible beauty standards to health. A healthy body that is capable of performing all kinds of tasks is much more fulfilling to its "owner" than a body that is thin and "beautiful" but too weak and emaciated to accomplish anything.

If America's obesity crisis is to be overcome, the fight against body-hate and ignorance is one of the first battles society will have to win. The obesity epidemic is real, threatens millions of people's health, and needs to be addressed. Discriminating against people for their excess weight or obesity, however, makes the epidemic worse. As long as people are harshly judged and blamed, excess weight and obesity go unrecognized as legitimate

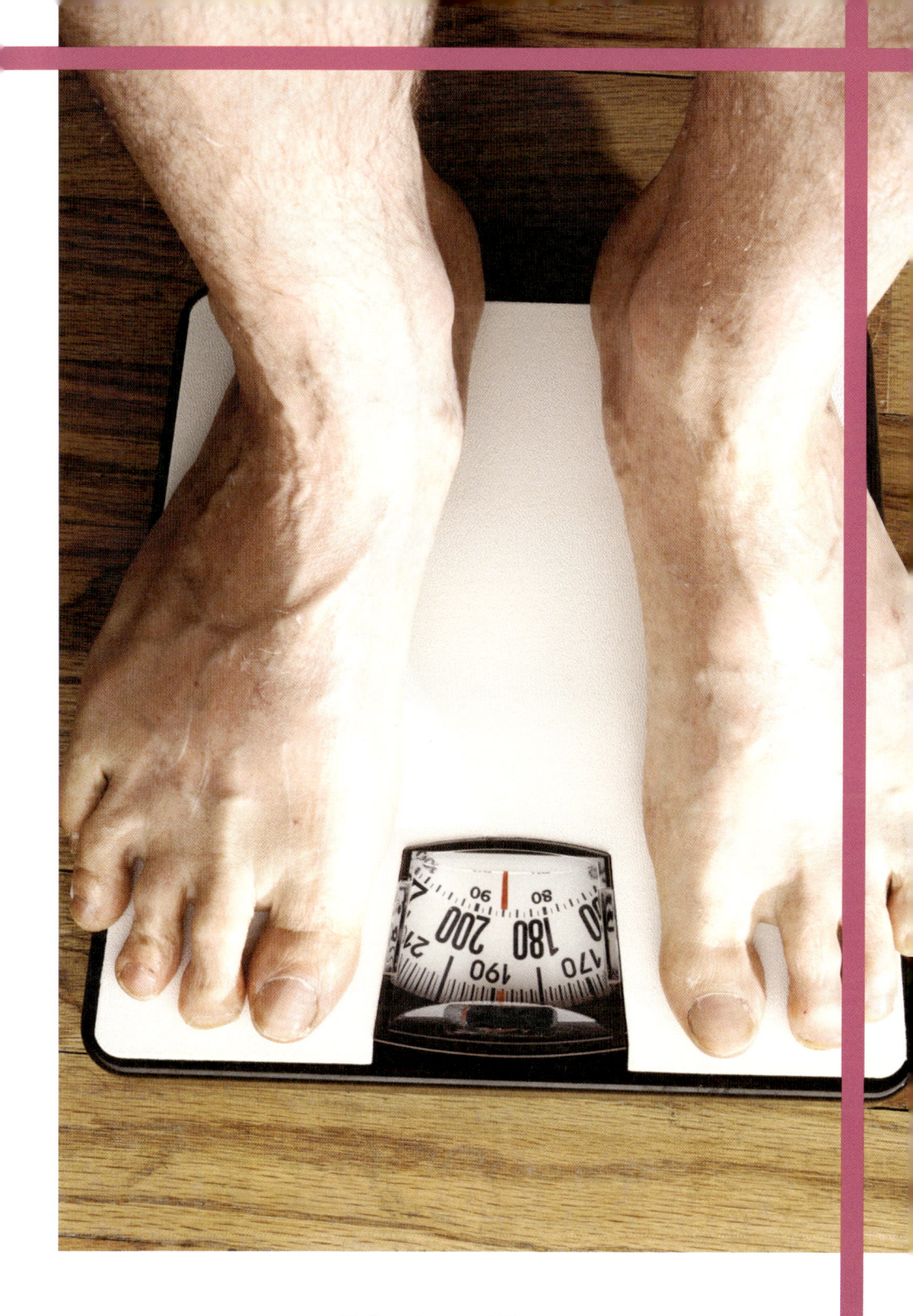

No Easy Answers

Research Project

Read the fifteen points of the Surgeon General's call to action, listed in this chapter. For each point, think of a way you can include the Surgeon General's advice in your own life. How can each item on the list make you, your friends, and your family healthier?

medical conditions and therefore remain untreated. And as long as we continue to judge those struggling with these conditions, we will ignore the part we all play (whether we struggle with our weight or not) in **perpetuating** lifestyles, practices, and attitudes that contribute to the epidemic.

Text-Dependent Questions:

1. What are four products that are a part of the weight-loss industry?
2. Do diets work? Why or why not?
3. What is "yo-yo" dieting? How has it helped the diet industry survive?
4. What are four of the Surgeon General's recommendations for a healthier lifestyle?
5. Why does unfairly judging those with obesity or overweight contribute to the obesity epidemic?

Series Glossary of Key Terms

Aerobic exercise: Activities that use large muscle groups (back, chest, and legs) to increase heart rate and breathing for an extended period of time, such as bicycling, brisk walking, running, and swimming. Federal guidelines recommend that adults get 150 to 300 minutes of aerobic activity a week.

Body mass index (BMI): A measure of body weight relative to height that uses a mathematical formula to get a score to determine if a person is underweight, at a normal weight, overweight, or obese. For adults, a BMI of 18.5 to 24.9 is considered healthy; a person with a BMI of 25 to 29.9 is considered overweight, and a person with a BMI of 30 or more is considered obese. BMI charts for children compare their height and weight to other children of their same sex and age.

Calorie: A unit of energy in food.

Carbohydrate: A type of food that is a major source of energy for your body. Your digestive system changes carbohydrates into blood glucose (sugar). Your body uses this sugar to make energy for cells, tissues, and organs, and stores any extra sugar in your liver and muscles for when it is needed. If there is more sugar than the body can use, it is stored as body fat.

Cholesterol: A fat-like substance that is made by your body and found naturally in animal foods such as dairy products, eggs, meat, poultry, and seafood. Foods high in cholesterol include dairy fats, egg yolks, and organ meats such as liver. Cholesterol is needed to carry out functions such as hormone and vitamin production, but too much can build up inside arteries, increasing the risk of heart disease.

Diabetes: A person with this disease has blood glucose—sugar—levels that are above normal levels. Insulin is a hormone that helps the glucose get into your cells to give them energy. Diabetes occurs when the body does not make enough insulin or does not use the insulin it makes. Over time, having too much sugar in your blood may cause serious problems. It may damage your eyes, kidneys, and nerves, and may cause heart disease and stroke. Regular physical activity, weight control, and healthy eating helps to control or prevent diabetes.

Diet: What a person eats and drinks. It may also be a type of eating plan.

Fat: A major source of energy in the diet that also helps the body absorb fat-soluble vitamins, such as vitamins A, D, E, and K.

High blood pressure: Blood pressure refers to the way blood presses against the blood vessels as it flows through them. With high blood pressure, the heart works harder, and the chances of a stroke, heart attack, and kidney problems are greater.

Metabolism: The process that occurs in the body to turn the food you eat into energy your body can use.

Nutrition: The process of the body using food to sustain life.

Obesity: Excess body fat that is more than 20 percent of what is considered to be healthy.

Overweight: Excess body fat that is more than 10 to 20 percent of what is considered to be healthy.

Portion size: The amount of a food served or eaten in one occasion. A portion is not a standard amount (it's different from a "serving size"). The amount of food it includes may vary by person and occasion.

Protein: One of the nutrients in food that provides calories to the body. Protein is an essential nutrient that helps build many parts of the body, including blood, bone, muscle, and skin. It is found in foods like beans, dairy products, eggs, fish, meat, nuts, poultry, and tofu.

Saturated fat: This type of fat is solid at room temperature. It is found in foods like full-fat dairy products, coconut oil, lard, and ready-to-eat meats. Eating a diet high in saturated fat can raise blood cholesterol and increase the risk of heart disease.

Serving size: A standard amount of a food, such as a cup or an ounce.

Stroke: When blood flow to your brain stops, causing brain cells to begin to die.

Trans fats: A type of fat produced when liquid fats (oils) are turned into solid fats through a chemical process called hydrogenation. Eating a large amount of trans fats raises blood cholesterol and increases the risk of heart disease.

Unsaturated fat: These healthier fats are liquid at room temperature. Vegetable oils are a major source of unsaturated fat. Other foods, such as avocados, fatty fish like salmon and tuna, most nuts, and olives are good sources of unsaturated fat.

Whole grains: Grains and grain products made from the entire grain seed; usually a good source of dietary fiber.

Further Reading

Bryan, Dale-Marie. *Obesity Discrimination*. New York: Rosen, 2008.

Dispoto, William. *Dangerous Toilets, Dollar Menus, Dirty Looks, and Discrimination: A Hard Look at Obesity in America*. Seattle, WA: CreateSpace, 2012.

Haslam, David W., Arya M. Sharma, and Carel W. le Roux. *Controversies in Obesity*. New York: Springer, 2014.

Kittler, Pamela Goyan. *Food and Culture*. Stamford, CT: Cengage, 2011.

Polan, Michael. *Food Rules: An Eater's Manual*. New York: Penguin, 2009.

———. *Supersized: Strange Tales from a Fast-Food Culture*. Milwaukie, OR: Dark Horse Comics, 2010.

Wilson, Charles and Eric Schlosser. *Chew on This: Everything You Don't Want to Know About Fast Food*. New York: HMH Books, 2013.

For More Information

Centers for Disease Control and Prevention: Overweight and Obesity
www.cdc.gov/obesity/index.html

The Civil Rights Act of 1964
www.archives.gov/education/lessons/civil-rights-act

Council on Size and Weight Discrimination
www.cswd.org

Harvard School of Public Health: Healthy Eating Plate
www.hsph.harvard.edu/nutritionsource/healthy-eating-plate

Mind on the Media
www.mindonthemedia.org

National Association to Advance Fat Acceptance
www.naafaonline.com/dev2

Obesity Information from MedlinePlus: A Service of the U.S. National Library of Medicine and the National Institutes of Health
www.nlm.nih.gov/medlineplus/obesity.html

Obesity Society
www.obesity.org

The Surgeon General's Call to Action to Prevent and Decrease Overweight and Obesity
www.surgeongeneral.gov/topics/obesity

TOLERANCE.ORG: A Project of the Southern Poverty Law Center
www.tolerance.org

Unites States Department of Agriculture: National Agricultural Library
fnic.nal.usda.gov

Publisher's note:
The websites listed on this page were active at the time of publication. The publisher is not responsible for websites that have changed their addresses or discontinued operation since the date of publication. The publisher will review and update the website list upon each reprint.

Index

access to goods and services 13, 15, 45, 51, 53–54, 81–83, 90
advertising 12, 58–63, 65, 67, 69
AIDS and HIV 45–47
attitude 16, 19, 31, 39, 55, 83, 90, 94, 97

barriers to eating well 48–51
body mass index (BMI) 26, 29–31, 38–39
body types 37–39
body-hate 11, 13, 94
bullying and BMI 75, 77

Civil Rights Act of 1964 18
consumer culture 56, 58

depression 31
diet industry 86–87, 89, 97
discrimination and obesity 11, 16–19, 21, 31, 38–39, 42, 55, 73, 75, 77–78, 80–83, 86, 89, 94,
discrimination in education, overweight and obesity and 73, 77–78
discrimination in employment, overweight and obesity and 73, 78–83
discrimination in social situations, overweight and obesity and 73–75

eating habits, evolution and 34, 36
economic factors of overweight and obesity 42, 44
education and overweight and obesity 43, 45, 51, 90, 94
exercise 31, 33, 36–39, 53–54, 65, 86

fast food 15, 34, 58–61, 63, 65, 67–69

Harvard School of Public Health healthy eating plate 34
health care, access to 51, 53–55, 90

left ventricular hypertrophy 29

Manheim, Camryn 82
McDonald's 60, 63
metabolism 22, 37–39
MyPlate 33

National Association to Advance Fat Acceptance (NAAFA) 80
National Institutes of Health (NIH) 30

obesity, prevalence of 47, 55, 93
obesity-related health risks 16, 20–21, 29–31, 38, 87

self-esteem 31, 77
smoking 31, 45–47, 55, 69
social stigmatization 8, 16, 74
stereotype 8, 19, 78
Surgeon General's Call to Action to Prevent and Decrease Overweight and Obesity 89–93

United States Department of Agriculture Food Guide Pyramid 33

Watts, Missy 78–80, 83
weight gain 19, 31–32, 34, 36, 38, 42, 45, 58, 87

"yo-yo" dieting 89, 97

Picture Credits

Andres Rodriguez | Dreamstime.com: p. 22
Banana Stock: p. 27
CDC: p. 46
Clipart.com: pp. 16, 18, 36, 37, 39, 54, 60, 67, 69, 83
Danil Chepko | Dreamstime.com: p. 84
Elenathewise - Fotolia.com: p. 66
Hemera: pp. 49, 50, 52, 59, 76, 79, 87, 92
Inger Anne Hulbækdal - Fotolia.com: p. 70
Jasmin Merdan - Fotolia.com: p. 61
Martinmark | Dreamstime.com: p. 97
Mikhail Kokhanchikov | Dreamstime.com: p. 8
Nina Vaclavova | Dreamstime.com: p. 12
Nyul | Dreamstime.com: p. 10
PhotoDisc: pp. 95, 96
Photos.com: pp. 61, 62, 64, 88, 91
Robwilson39 | Dreamstime.com: p. 68
Imagesource: pp. 14, 17, 18–19, 25, 72, 74
Stockbyte: pp. 28, 35, 43
USDA: p. 32
Vladmax | Dreamstime.com: p. 40
Wavebreakmedia Ltd | Dreamstime.com: p. 56

About the Author & the Consultant

Autumn Libal received her degree from Smith College in Northampton, MA. A former water-aerobics instructor, she now dedicates herself exclusively to writing for young people. Other Mason Crest series she has contributed to include PSYCHIATRIC DISORDERS: DRUGS & PSYCHOLOGY FOR THE MIND AND BODY, YOUTH WITH SPECIAL NEEDS and the SCIENCE OF YOUTH AND WELL-BEING. She has also written health-related articles for *New Moon: The Magazine for Girls and Their Dreams*.

Dr. Victor F. Garcia is the co-director of the Comprehensive Weight Management Center at Cincinnati Children's Hospital Medical Center. He is a board member of Discover Health of Greater Cincinnati, a fellow of the American College of Surgeons, and a two-time winner of the Martin Luther King Humanitarian Award.